TRYST

WITH

DESTINY

Roma Dhingra

DEDICATION

For my children
Rowena and Neil

ACKNOWLEDGEMENTS

I was born in New Delhi, India, in 1946, a year before its partition from Pakistan. My father had been sent from Lahore to Calcutta to help quell the riots in Calcutta in February of 1946. He advised my mother to move to New Delhi immediately as he suspected a partition of India into two states was imminent.

She did, and I was born a few months after her move. Many of their relatives and friends moved from Lahore after the partition of India and Pakistan in 1947, only to find themselves homeless in New Delhi. My parents invited them to stay with us for as long as it took for them to find a home. We lived like a very large family, and for me, it was fun.

As a child I never understood about the horrors of the partition of 1947. All across India, communities that had coexisted for centuries turned against each other. Migrants, from one country to the other, faced massacres, abductions, bodily mutilations, and sexual violations. Millions died and thousands were left homeless during the months after the partition. The ones who made it across safely wanted to forget about this period and rebuild their lives.

I grew up at a time when patriotism was high. Indians were encouraged to wear clothes made from *khadi* (homespun cotton) or pure silk. Students carried the tricolor flag, stuck on a toothpick, in their pencil boxes. Many of the pencils were tricolored. Every morning the school assembly began with the national anthem. The country's energy was focused on rehabilitating the citizens of India and making the country one great nation.

The stories of my parents and relatives seemed like interesting, scary stories one tells at night. When I shared their stories about the events that occurred during the haphazard partition of India and Pakistan with the writers at the Writers' Workshop, they were not familiar with this time in history and urged me to write about it.

Tryst with Destiny, a fictionalized love story, set during the time of the 1947 partition, is the result. Without the encouragement and helpful suggestions of the writers at the Writers' Workshop, this story would not have been written. I thank them all. Writing the story brought back many memories of a special time in my life.

I'd especially like to thank Caroline Corser, Saundra Sheffer, Pat Sheehan, Judy Vigo, and Wayne Tennille for all their extra help.

I'd like to thank my sister, Asha Marathe. Her encouragement and help awakened my memories of the partition. I thank my aunt, Vimal Nikore, for sharing her stories about her life in Bhakkar, and her time at a refugee camp. Thanks to Veena Menda for sharing the story of how she migrated from Sind to Bombay, (now Mumbai). Thanks to Bhaskar Bose for helping with the mind boggling task of page layout and formatting and a special thanks to my parents, and my in-laws for sharing their stories of the partition.

TIMELINE OF MAJOR EVENTS LISTED IN THIS BOOK

1946

August 14   The Muslim League announces *Direct Action Day*- a strike against the ruling that India will not be divided

August 16-18 The announcement of *Direct Action Day* results in violence in Calcutta

1947

March 6   Muslim crowds and the Muslim National Guards attack Hindus and Sikhs in West Punjab

March 23   New Viceroy, Louis Mountbatten wife, Edwina, arrives

June 3   The plan to partition India and Pakistan is announced

August 9   News that Radcliffe turned in his recommendations for the partition. Public is informed that the British will transfer its power to India and Pakistan at midnight on August 15. The new boundaries to be announced on August 14

August 14   Pakistan Independence Day

August 15   India Independence Day

October 22	Pakistani rebels invade Independent Kashmir
October 26	V.P. Menon flies to Jammu to get a signature from Maharaja of Kashmir to sign an instrument of succession to India

1948

January 30	Mahatma Gandhi assassinated by Hindu extremist, Godse

1950

January 26	Inauguration of the Republic of India

Tryst with Destiny Speech by Prime Minister Jawaharlal Nehru on India's Independence from the British

With the clock striking the midnight hour on the 14-15th of August 1947, India was 'to awake to freedom' from the British and a partition from Pakistan. The Constituent Assembly to whom power was to be transferred began its sitting at 11 p.m. It was a historic and memorable occasion in the life of the Constituent Assembly. After an address by the President, Jawaharlal Nehru made his now famous **Tryst with Destiny** *speech. He called upon the members to take a solemn pledge to serve India and her people.*

Long years ago we made a **tryst with destiny**, and now the time comes when we shall redeem our pledge, not wholly or in full measure, but very substantially.

At the stroke of the midnight hour, when the world sleeps, India will awake to life and freedom. A moment comes, which comes but rarely in history, when we step out from the old to the new, when an age ends, and when the soul of a nation, long suppressed, finds utterance.

It is fitting that at this solemn moment we take the pledge of dedication to the service of India and her people and to the still larger cause of humanity with some pride

At the dawn of history India started on her unending quest, and trackless centuries, which are filled with her striving and the grandeur of her success and her failures. Through good and ill fortunes alike she has never lost sight of that quest or forgotten the ideals, which gave her strength. We end today a period of ill fortunes and India discovers herself again.

The achievement we celebrate today is but a step, an opening of opportunity, to the greater triumphs and achievements that await us. Are we brave enough and wise enough to grasp this opportunity and accept the challenge of the future?

Freedom and power bring responsibility. The responsibility rests upon this assembly, a sovereign body representing the sovereign people of India. Before the birth of freedom we have endured all the pains of labour and our hearts are heavy with the memory of this sorrow. Some of those pains continue even now. Nevertheless, the past is over and it is the future that beckons to us now.

That future is not one of ease or resting but of incessant striving so that we might fulfill the pledges we have so often taken and the one we shall take today. The service of India means the service of the millions who suffer. It means the ending of poverty and ignorance and disease and inequality of opportunity.

The ambition of the greatest man of our generation has been to wipe every tear from every eye. That may be beyond us, but as long as there are tears and suffering, so long our work will not be over.

And so we have to labour and to work, and work hard, to give reality to our dreams. Those dreams are for India, but they are also for the world, for all the nations and peoples are too closely knit together today for anyone of them to imagine that it can live apart.

Peace has been said to be indivisible; so is freedom, so is prosperity now, and so also is disaster in this one world that can no longer be split into isolated fragments.

To the people of India, whose representatives we are, we make an appeal to join us with faith and confidence in this great adventure. This is no time for petty and destructive criticism, no time for ill will or blaming others. We have to build the noble mansion of free India where all her children may dwell.

The appointed day has come - the day appointed by destiny - and India stands forth again, after long slumber and struggle, awake, vital, free and independent. The past clings on to us still in some measure and we have to do much before we redeem the pledges we have so often taken. Yet the turning point is past, and history begins anew for us, the history which we shall live and act and others will write about.

It is a fateful moment for us in India, for all Asia and for the world. A new star rises, the star of freedom in the east, a new hope comes into being, a vision long cherished materializes. May the star never set and that hope never be betrayed!

We rejoice in that freedom, even though clouds surround us, and many of our people are sorrow-stricken and difficult problems encompass us. But freedom brings responsibilities and burdens and we have to face them in the spirit of a free and disciplined people.

On this day our first thoughts go to the architect of this freedom, the father of our nation, who, embodying the old spirit of India, held aloft the torch of freedom and lighted up the darkness that surrounded us.

We have often been unworthy followers of his and have strayed from his message, but not only we but succeeding generations will remember this message and bear the imprint in their hearts of this great son of India, magnificent in his faith and strength and courage and humility. We shall never allow that torch of freedom to be blown out, however high the wind or stormy the tempest.

Our next thoughts must be of the unknown volunteers and soldiers of freedom who, without praise or reward, have served India even unto death.

We think also of our brothers and sisters who have been cut off from us by political boundaries and who unhappily cannot share at present in the freedom that has come. They are of us and will remain of us whatever may happen, and we shall be sharers in their good and ill fortune alike.

The future beckons to us. Whither do we go and what shall be our endeavour? To bring freedom and opportunity to the common man, to the peasants and workers of India; to fight and end poverty 'and ignorance and disease; to build up a prosperous, democratic and progressive nation, and to create social, economic and political institutions which will ensure justice and fullness of life to every man and woman.

We have hard work ahead. There is no resting for any one of us till we redeem our pledge in full, till we make all the people of India what destiny intended them to be.

We are citizens of a great country, on the verge of bold advance, and we have to live up to that high standard. All of us, to whatever religion we may belong, are equally the children of India with equal rights, privileges and obligations. We cannot encourage communalism or narrow-mindedness, for no nation can be great whose people are narrow in thought or in action.

To the nations and peoples of the world we send greetings and pledge ourselves to cooperate with them in furthering peace, freedom and democracy.

And to India, our much-loved motherland, the ancient, the eternal and the ever-new, we pay our reverent homage and we bind ourselves afresh to her service. *Jai Hind* (Victory for India).

(Reference: Wikipedia; The Guardian)

TRYST WITH DESTINY

Murad walked out of the bank with his briefcase. His driver awaited in his white Triumph parked right in front. He got into the car and told his driver to switch the radio station to the news. While listening to a report on the conflict between the British, and the Muslims and the Hindus, he froze.

"Good evening. This is Saif Khan, Radio Lahore, bringing you the latest evening news on this day of August 14, 1946. Mohammed Ali Jinnah, the leader of the Muslim League has stated that he wants India divided. He wants an independent country for the Muslims. Today he sponsored a *Direct Action Day* – a strike against the recent ruling that India would not be divided.

"Mr. Jinnah says, 'We shall have India divided or we shall have India destroyed. Pakistan is worth taking ten million Muslim lives.'

"Gandhiji and the Congress party leaders feel that India should remain intact because people of all religions can coexist. Mohammed Ali Jinnah feels this is a Utopian ideal. An undivided India would only result in a prolonged civil war. Mr. Jinnah's instigation of the strike has resulted in riots and burning down of houses. So far, four thousand Hindus, Sikhs, and Muslims have been killed in Calcutta, and one hundred thousand have been left homeless. This could lead to retaliation and more violence. Mahatma Gandhi has implored the Indian people to continue to unite in peaceful opposition to the British rule. I will keep you updated."

Murad couldn't understand it. In Lahore, where he lived, the Christians, Muslims, Hindus, Sikhs, and Zoroastrians, lived peacefully together. Lahore was an international city.

Murad had moved to Lahore after his years of studying law at King's College and business at the London School of Economics in England. He had found a job at his bank soon after he married his wife, Amber. He was twenty-four years old then, and she was twenty.

Their son, Neil, was born a year later and their daughter, Nina, was born two years after that. They had lived here for eighteen years. He enjoyed his work as the president of National Gridley's Bank. He had reached that position at the young age of forty-two. Amber had gone back to college to complete a Bachelor of Education degree. Neil had recently graduated from high school with honors.

When the driver parked in front of the house, Murad rushed in and called out to his wife.

"Amber, Amber, where are you?" Amber and their son, Neil came running down the stairs.

"Did you hear the news?" Murad asked.

"Oh, that." His wife smiled, not noticing his disturbed demeanor. "But how did you hear it? We just got Neil's admission letter from Cambridge University this morning."

"I'm in, Papa!" Neil beamed.

Murad hugged his son and kissed his head. "I am so proud of you, *beta*! I know you will excel there." Then he turned to both of them. "I have some other news as well. Jinnah proclaimed today, *Direct Action Day,* a time to revolt against *India Undivided* between the Muslims and the Hindus. He wants his own Muslim country but he is only instigating the Muslims against the Hindus."

"He is forgetting about the Sikhs and Christians, Jews, Parsis, Baha'is, Buddhists, and Jains." Amber pointed out. "The British can't just divide India like that. People of all religions live all over India. Which area will they give to the Hindus and which to the Muslims? It doesn't make any sense. Our neighbors, Sayed and Najma, are like our family. Our children are close friends. We have so many friends of various faiths. We love each other because of all the differences. I don't want us to leave our beloved Lahore and move to a strange new place."

Murad put his arms around Amber and Neil. "Maybe we won't have to, but we need to be prepared," Murad comforted. "We will go to Shimla where my parents live. Your aunt will be there as well. Later we can move to New Delhi. There is a branch of my bank in New Delhi. I will look for a position there.

"I will talk to some people who might have inside information. You may remember the British promised India her independence when we sent our troops to fight for the British during World War I. One hundred thousand Indian troops were killed fighting the British war in 1918. But the British reneged on their promise. As a result, the *Indian National Congress* refused to support Britain in World War II."

Murad continued, "Mohammed Ali Jinnah, and his League, supported them. The British threw all the Hindu protesters in jail but now, because of the Muslim League participation in the second war, the British owe Jinnah. The West is talking about self-government and

3

an end to colonialism. Everyone wants to see an independent India, but a divided India? I hope not."

"Remember when Hari had called Sheila six months ago to warn her of something like this?" Amber asked.

Murad nodded. "Yes. He was in Calcutta, sent there to quell the riots and looting. He told her to move to Delhi with her children, as a partition of India was imminent. Hari was badly injured when he fell from the roof of a burning building."

"Sheila wrote to tell me Hari had recovered now. But she warned me to plan for a move soon."

"I know," Murad replied. "You told me but it seemed unbelievable because Lahore remains relatively untouched by political intrigues. I will let you know what I find out tomorrow."

***

Mahnoor, the maid, bustled in to tell them dinner was on the table. Mahnoor was a slim, dark-skinned, woman. Her teeth were stained red from chewing *paan*, a mixture of betel nuts, tobacco and flavorings wrapped up in a heart-shaped betel leaf. "Why are you all looking so worried?" she asked.

"The British are thinking of dividing the country between the Hindus and Muslims," replied Neil.

"If that happens," said Mahnoor, "I am going with you and your family. I might be a Musalman, but I have taken care of you since you and Nina were babies. I am not leaving now."

Amber knew Mahnoor's plan wouldn't be possible, if India was in fact divided.

4

That night, Amber lay awake thinking about what could happen. She also wondered if her family in Bhakkar knew about the current situation. Her father was a criminal attorney. He must know. What would happen to them? The next morning she booked a call to Bhakkar and waited to get connected. Half an hour later, the operator called her to tell her she had a connection. Amber's seventeen-year-old sister, Aparna answered.

"Aparna, how are all of you?"

"We are fine. But every day we hear explosions. I place cotton in my ears to block the noise. I am frightened."

"Is *Ammi* there? May I speak to her?"

Her mother must have been close by, because she answered right away.

"*Ammi,*" Amber said, "Murad says the British are going to divide India into two countries. You might have to move."

"We are going to be fine, Amber. We will move to your sister's house until the rioting subsides. Her house is like a fortress, and it is huge. We have built makeshift bridges of wood and rope, leading from one rooftop to the next, all the way to her house. Instead of walking through the winding lanes, we will use the rooftops as a shortcut. If there is a problem we can take shelter at her house. Her family has assured us that we can use their *haveli*, as a camp for all of us, and any other neighbors, till the rioting stops."

"*Ammi*, you don't understand," Amber said urgently. "If Bhakkar does not remain a part of India, you cannot stay."

"Why? Most of the people who live around here are peace loving. It is just some *goondas* and rioters that are causing trouble. Even if India is divided I am sure we can still stay here."

"*Ammi*, you all need to leave. Your lives are in danger. Please talk to Papa. Murad has suggested that the children and I move to Shimla as soon as we have definite news of the partition." Amber hung up the phone. She was worried.

***

Murad returned home that evening, his brow furrowed. This time Amber was waiting for him. Murad took her hands and guided her to the sofa. "The riots in Calcutta are continuing," he said. "Britain is struggling after World War II. Hitler's army has left the economy of Britain in shambles. Our freedom movement is very strong, and Britain can't afford a war with a large country like India."

Amber's body stilled as she listened.

Murad sighed, "The talk is that India will get its independence, but the country will be divided. The British will give Jinnah a homeland for the Muslims. But no one has any idea where the dividing line will be. There are Muslims and Hindus spread out all over the country."

"West Punjab and East Bengal has mostly Muslims," Amber said.

Murad nodded in agreement. "That's true, and Lahore is in West Punjab. But nothing will happen for at least another year."

"I have heard the new British Labor Party is against colonialism," Amber said. "World power has shifted from Western Europe to America and Russia. I heard on the radio that America and Russia are ideologically opposed to colonialism."

Murad nodded. He had heard similar stories.

Amber shook her head. "What can we do?"

"There is a very small chance that India will not be divided," Murad mused. "I still have faith in the Unionist government of Khizr Hayat Tiwana. He has many Hindus, Sikhs, and Muslims in his cabinet, and he is strongly opposed to a separate Muslim state. Let's wait and see. Even if we stay, start the preparation for a move, just in case. We may be here for a year or two or just a few months. We will move to Shimla first and stay with my parents. From there we will move to New Delhi. I will ask for a transfer to our branch there."

Murad was relieved after talking to Amber. She had handled the news with her usual calm, and with understanding.

***

Amber and Murad

Amber remembered her visit to Shimla when she met Murad for the first time. She was staying with her mother's youngest sister, Vimla. Her aunt moved to Shimla every summer with her husband and family.

Shimla was the summer capital of India. From May to October all the government offices moved to Shimla, away from the burning heat of the plains. Amber was nineteen years old. She had been playing cricket with her cousins when she saw Murad watching her over the hedge. His eyes seemed to absorb her dark auburn hair, warm amber colored eyes, and her glowing complexion. His sister, Mona, standing by his side, yelled to Amber's cousins, to ask if she could play with them. Amber's cousins invited them both over. Murad and his sister, Mona, walked over through a gap in the hedge and joined their cricket game.

Amber found out that Murad was visiting from London where he attended the London School of Economics. His tall, handsome, and sophisticated demeanor attracted her. He was about six feet tall. He had hazel-grey eyes and dark brown hair. His nose had a hook, but it did not detract from his looks.

Later, when Murad had a chance to talk to Amber alone, he asked what she liked to do, how she spent her spare time, and how many siblings she had. Nobody else had shown such interest in her. She was flattered and excited.

They continued to see and talk to each other every day. Sometimes they walked up Mall Road with his sister, Mona, and Amber's cousins, Natasha and Anil, to buy ice cream or a snack. Murad told her all about his life in London. He had completed his law degree and had joined the London School of Economics for another year of study. Amber was in her second year of college and also had another year to go before she completed her undergraduate studies in Home Economics.

Murad asked her what she wanted to do after she completed her undergraduate studies.

"I would like to be a teacher," she said. "I would like to get my B.Ed. and then get my master's degree so I can teach at a university."

Murad stopped to turn to her. "You know, your air of quiet fragility is quite deceptive. You are actually quite strong and determined about what you want out of life," he mused.

"My parents have always sheltered me from the outside world, but I know what I want to do with my life," Amber agreed. "They have known you for nineteen years, and they don't know you as well as I do," Murad said with a smile.

"What about you?" Amber teased. "You want everyone to think you are easygoing. But your mind is always churning. You are always focused on what you need to do next."

"Yes," Murad replied, looking at her. "I know what I'd like to do next."

They started taking walks together and enjoyed an easy camaraderie. Amber's aunt liked Murad and encouraged the relationship. One day when they walked through a wooded hillside, Amber asked Murad what his name meant.

"Don't you know? It's an Urdu word. It means 'wish.' He grinned and winked at her. "I'm every girl's wish come true!" Amber laughed. He loved it when she laughed. It had a light tinkling sound.

"I know why you were named Amber," Murad smiled. "Your eyes glow like amber, and they are so beautiful." Her face flushed.

"You're shy!" Murad chuckled.

"Actually, I was named Ambar which means, 'sky,' but on my first day at school, when I told my teacher my name, she spelled it A-m-b-e-r. My parents and I never bothered to correct her spelling. Now all my school certificates have that spelling!"

"I'm glad," replied Murad. He grinned. Your name always reminds me of your eyes.

9

A few weeks before Murad was due to return to London, Amber walked out to the front yard, deep in thought. She would miss him. She wondered if she should share with Murad how she felt about him. She shook her head, embarrassed by her thoughts. How could she do that? Murad might have no feelings for her. But he seemed to like her. *Then it is up to him to make the first move, you idiot,* an inner voice reprimanded her. She covered her face with her hands. *What should I do? I must talk to him,* Amber thought just as she heard a movement near her. It was Murad standing near the boundary hedge beckoning to her. She looked towards him.

"Come over, I want to show you something."

Amber crossed through the gap in the hedge.

"Come inside."

She had never been inside his house. Murad guided her to an actual ballroom. A black box lay on a table by the wall. It was lying open. On the inside of the lid was the picture of a dog listening to a megaphone. Above it were the words, *His Master's Voice.* There was a crank handle inserted on one side to wind up the box. At the center was a short spindle, and a metal arm on the side.

"Oh, a gramophone!" exclaimed Amber

"Yes," said Murad smiling. "Do you dance?"

"No," she blushed. "I've seen some people dancing at the club, but I have never danced."

"Come, I'll teach you the waltz."

"No, your parents would not like that."

"They aren't here. Nor is my sister. They are visiting friends. Come, I will teach you."

10

He put a record on the gramophone and wound it up. He then placed the metal arm at the beginning of the record. "It is called the *Blue Danube Waltz*. I brought it with me from London. It is beautiful. I can listen to it over and over again. Okay, place your left hand on my shoulder." Murad placed his right hand on her back. He held out his left hand, and Amber placed her hand in his.

"Come, 1, 2, 3…1,2,3, …boom-tick-tick."

Amber followed his lead. Murad whirled her around the room. He stole her breath away. She was falling in love with this wonderful man. He pulled her a little closer. She rested her head on his shoulder. Time seemed to stand still. She floated around the room with the music. The music began to slow down. The box needed to be re-wound. Murad did not let go of her when he leaned over to rewind the gramophone, and change the record.

Now the music was livelier. Murad swung her around the room faster.

"Heaven, I'm in Heaven
And my heart beats so that I can hardly speak;
And I seem to find the happiness I seek
When we are out together dancing cheek to cheek…"

At the end of the dance, Murad pulled her to him and kissed her forehead. "I love you, Amber," he murmured.

"I love you, too," she replied breathlessly. "I wanted to tell you, but I am glad you said it first. I don't know if I could have been bold enough to say the words to you."

Murad captured her face with his hands. "In two weeks, I have to return to London, but I don't want to leave you," Murad whispered. "I know if I leave you now, your parents will probably get you engaged to a suitable man even before you complete college. I can't let that happen. I have loved you from the moment I saw you, and I don't want to lose you."

"I don't either," Amber whispered.

"Let's get engaged now and we can get married next year after I return," Murad suggested. "I know you will graduate a few months before I do."

"But how? Will your parents agree? What will my aunt, Vimla, think?"

"Don't worry about any of them," he said confidently. "I will talk to my parents. I know they like you. My sister, Mona, likes you too. They will talk to your aunt and uncle."

That night, Amber could not sleep. She knew she loved Murad deeply but she worried about how his parents would react. She wasn't so worried about her aunt and uncle. She knew they liked Murad.

She held her breath when she saw Murad's parents walk over to her aunt's house the next day. She hid in the next room to try to hear what was being said. The voices were muffled, but then she heard laughter and she could breathe again. Her aunt called out to her. When Amber walked in shyly, her aunt came over to give her a hug.

"Do you like Murad?" her aunt whispered, and Amber nodded. Murad's parents hugged her too.

"We would love to have you as our daughter-in-law, Amber. Would you like to marry Murad?"

Amber bowed her head and nodded shyly.

They called Murad in. He had been waiting outside, impatient to hear their decision.

Congratulations were shared, along with sweets. Amber's parents, in Bhakkar, were informed. Her aunt told them that Murad was a wonderful match for Amber. His parents were good people, Vimla told them, and they had nothing to worry about. Amber's parents were delighted. The engagement date was set for that weekend. It would give each family a chance to get rings. There was a lot of teasing from the cousins and Murad's sister, Mona. But it was all in fun.

Amber remembered her engagement ceremony. Murad had looked so handsome in a navy blue suit, pale blue shirt and a maroon tie. He had ordered this suit to take back with him to London. Because of time restraints, Amber's aunt and uncle had paid for it and given it to Murad as their gift. Murad's mother had presented Amber her own engagement *sari*. She had a new blouse made to fit Amber. On the day of the engagement, Murad's mother had brought the maroon and gold *sari,* gold jewelry, heeled-sandals and an anklet on a gold tray. Then she took Amber to her room to dress her in the outfit and jewelry she had brought. Murad waited patiently and endured the teasing of the younger ones. Finally, Amber was escorted out.

After the formalities were over, it was time for the ring ceremony. Murad slowly turned towards her and came down on one knee. This was not at all the tradition, and everyone was surprised.

"Will you marry me, Amber?" he asked holding Amber's hand in his.

Amber smiled in relief, "Yes," she replied, blushing shyly. The guests cheered.

13

Amber's cousin, Natasha, wanted to look at the engagement ring. "This ring is beautiful. It is so unusual. Which stone is this?" Natasha asked.

"It's a clear Baltic Amber, surrounded by diamonds," Murad explained, smiling. "The amber matches Amber's beautiful eyes."

Everyone teased both of them about Murad being such a romantic. Sweets were passed around. Murad offered Amber a sweet *laddu*. She took a bite and stuffed the rest into Murad's mouth. Everybody laughed.

The night before Murad was to leave for London, he asked Amber to meet him outside her house. The rest of the family had retired for the night. They sat outside and talked, holding hands, till the first ray of light began to show. They parted, hugging each other and making promises to write to each other.

***

They kept their promises. Amber wrote about her life in Bhakkar and its very elaborate celebrations of festivals, like *Dussehra*. She told Murad about riding on colorfully, bedecked camels and watching the burning of the demon king, *Ravana*. She told him about the carnival and dances that she participated in during the spring festival of *Basant*. The people of the town wore yellow clothes to celebrate spring because of the color of the yellow mustard flowers that were in bloom. Sometimes she illustrated her letters with pen sketches.

Murad wrote back about his life in London, about his studies, and some of his friendships.

Amber wrote about her boat rides on the canal, which took her family to their date orchards. She also told him of the disparity among the lives of the people who lived in Bhakkar. One part of the city had the large brick houses like her father's. On the other side there was extreme poverty. People lived in mud huts. But most of the families enjoyed fresh milk from their own cows.

Murad wrote about the plays he had seen and the dismal weather that London was experiencing. Both were far removed from each other's lifestyles, but they enjoyed connecting through these letters. It made their separation more bearable.

A year later, Murad and Amber married in Bhakkar. From there, they moved to Lahore where Murad went to work for a bank. Amber decided to study for another year. She received a B.Ed. (Bachelor of Education) degree. She was a qualified teacher, but she never worked as one. Her life was full. She and Murad had friends, with varied interests, who visited often.

While managing the housework, caring for her children, and entertaining guests, she had also discovered a new talent. She found that she had a flair for designing unique and beautiful jewelry. She had designed most of her own. When people saw her jewelry, they asked where she bought it. She told them that she designed her own. Many friends and acquaintances asked her to design something for them, and then, just by word of mouth, news of her talent spread among the local aristocratic circle. She hired two craftsmen to work for her, and her creations were called *Amber's Designs.*

A famous painter, Ambika, sought her out to design jewelry for her. Ambika was part French and part Indian, and though she traveled to both countries frequently, her heart belonged to India. She loved to paint portraits of the poor, the street urchins, and the villagers. Ambika had received many awards for her art in Europe, and the people of Lahore embraced her with pride. She was a favorite of journalists and photographers. She was not just beautiful. She was breathtakingly stunning.

One day, she breezed into Amber's house, her pale blue chiffon sari billowing around her. Amber recognized Ambika because she had seen her photos in the newspapers frequently. Ambika introduced herself and told Amber how much she admired her jewelry designs. Their friendship had developed from there. They liked each other immediately. Amber designed a few necklaces and earrings for Ambika. She had also designed matching rings.

Ambika painted a portrait of Neil and Nina who sat for her in their living room. Neil had a protective arm around his sister. Ambika called it *Siblings* and gave it to Murad and Amber as a gift. Their friendship grew over the years. Ambika loved to shock Amber, but Amber soon got used to that. Once she asked Amber how many men she'd had sexual relations with. Amber shook her head wryly.

"Just Murad. And you?"

"Oh, so many. How else would I be able to feel the beauty of form, the subtlety of color, the quality of line?"

"So you know how to feel the color and form and line of men. How do you feel the form and beauty of a woman?" Amber asked, teasing. "Your paintings of women are sensual and alluring."

"Oh, I've made love to women as well," she

16

replied casually, looking directly at Amber to see if she had finally shocked her.

When she saw the shock factor had not worked, Ambika continued, "You're an artist, too. Your jewelry designs are beautiful. Where do you find your creativity? Haven't you ever thought of exploring?"

"I get my thrill from looking at nature. I designed the bracelet you are wearing. Look at it. It was inspired by a twig I found in the garden. I look at the flowers, insects, birds, the sun, and the stars. I get real pleasure from that. I get my inspiration and creativity from nature," Amber explained.

One day Amber asked Ambika why she loved India so much. Didn't she miss the European lifestyle?

Ambika laughed. "There are such wonderful, such beautiful things in India, so many unexploited pictorial possibilities, that it is a pity that so few of us have looked for them and much less interpreted them," she explained. "I love the simplicity of the villagers and I love the colors."

"But you are famous in Europe. So many artists live there. Don't you miss that?" Amber quizzed.

"I am more famous here. Europe belongs to Picasso, Matisse and many others. India belongs only to me."

***

Lahore 1946-47
Every evening, families were glued to their radios listening to the news. Daily there was news of one uprising or another. But most were on the eastern side of the country, in and around Bengal. The massacre in Calcutta following the pronouncement of *Direct Action*

17

Day had shocked everyone. On August 16, 1946 people opened their newspapers to find large printed advertisements inside them.

"Today Muslims of India dedicate their lives and all
they possess to the cause of freedom.
Today let every Muslim swear in the name of Allah to
resist aggression.
Direct action is now their only course.
Because they offered peace but peace was spurned.
They honored their word but they were betrayed.
They claimed Liberty but were offered Thraldom.
Now might alone can secure their right."

What followed was the most horrifying religious riot of the twentieth century. Five to ten thousand Calcutta residents lay dead and fifteen thousand injured. Muslims, and Hindus killed each other with an intensity and ferocity that shocked.

LIFE magazine, in a two-page photo spread, titled "The Vultures of Calcutta," featured the stark pictures of the aftermath of the riots. Now each religious faction was wary of the other. This incident took place in the east, but Punjab and Sind were equally in danger.

"Good evening. This is Saif Khan, Radio Lahore. On this day of March 6, 1947, Muslim crowds and the *Muslim National Guards* systematically attacked Hindus and Sikhs in Western Punjab for the first time. Three thousand are said to be dead in the Rawalpindi area. Lord Mountbatten has been sent as the next Viceroy of India to bring about peace in the nation."

The next morning, Amber, and her family were suddenly awakened by what sounded like fire crackers and shouts of people crying *"Nara ek-Takhbir*, shout out loud *Allah hu Akbar, God is great."* The Hindus were shouting back *"Hari, Har, Mahadev,"* the other names for the gods, Brahma, Vishnu, and Shiva. The Sikhs shouted *"Bole son Nihal Sat Sri Akal,* let's all say, eternal is the holy, great, timeless, lord." The police came to disperse the crowd.

On March 23, 1947 the new Viceroy, Louis Mountbatten, and his beautiful wife, Edwina, arrived. The riots stopped for a while.

In a speech in the capital city of New Delhi, Mountbatten announced that the British planned to transfer their power to the people of India on June 15, 1948. India would remain in the British Commonwealth, but it could appoint its own ruling government. He would remain in India as the Governor General until all operations were running smoothly.

There was a sigh of relief all over the country. The rulers of the princely states went back to their usual routines. The five hundred and ninety-five princes of their small states did not want to join some big, conglomerated country. They had been fine under the noninterference of a British overlord. A few months of relative peace followed.

Life took on a relative normality. Murad and Amber met their friends at the Gymkhana Club. Their neighbors, Sayed and Najma came along frequently. Ambika was usually there with her husband, Eric Jeffers. She had married, a Fulbright Scholar, who had come from Yale to do research in Lahore. He would be in the country for two years and then return to America

19

with his beautiful bride. Ambika continued to paint, and her paintings, which had originally been influenced by the art of Gauguin, and Renoir, now took on an originality of their own. Her paintings were displayed at the National Museum of Art both in Lahore and New Delhi.

Conversations among their friends had changed subtly. Instead of discussions of market trends, art, music, jewelry, or daily problems, topics became more political.

Mahnoor and some of the other neighborhood maids sat outside on a grassy patch chewing *paan* and discussing the country's situation.

"In my uncle's village, some *goondas*, criminals, kidnapped some of the young women there," one said. "He says they probably raped them and killed them afterwards or used them as servants. The police have the report and are searching for the *goondas*."

"So often the police are involved in the kidnapping," another pointed out.

"Oh *sache badsha, mehir kar,* have mercy! Shocking things are happening. Either the police cannot do anything or they don't want to. Several bodies have been found strewn in the gutters."

"Were they Hindus?" questioned a maid, horrified.

"Hindus, Muslims, Sikhs, Christians, Parsis, who can tell?" replied the first.

"Brother is killing brother. Oh Allah have mercy! Times are changing, and not for the good," muttered Mahnoor.

"Jinnah, Nehru, Gandhiji, and Patel are stirring up trouble for all of us."

The friendships among some friends became closer, tighter somehow, because of the tenuous situation. But other relationships were ruled by fear and distrust.

***

New Delhi April 1947, Hari and Sheila

Hari walked into his house after work. His wife, Sheila, held the door open for him.

"Sheila, I received a letter from Murad in Lahore," he told her. "He says that they may have to leave Lahore and move to New Delhi now. He will come with his family. He asked if he and his family could stay with us until he finds a house."

"Of course they can stay with us," replied Sheila. "Summer is approaching fast. We will soon be sleeping in the central courtyard to stay cool. We will simply add four folding beds. They can share our room and bathroom to change and bathe."

Hari nodded. "Oh, by the way, we will have four guests for dinner tonight." Hari frequently surprised Sheila with unexpected guests. Over the years, she had become prepared for such events. She had a refrigerator now, so she could prepare food in advance and freeze it.

"Who?" Sheila inquired.

"Steven Davis and his wife. You haven't met them as yet. They arrived in New Delhi, from England, two weeks ago. Steven works with me. And you already know Kulwant and his wife," replied Hari. "I'll freshen up. May I have a cup of tea with jam toast?"

Sheila nodded and went to the kitchen to tell the cook to get tea and toast ready.

The evening proved to be quite interesting. Steven was reserved and very polite, but his friendly, talkative, wife joked about her problems dealing with the servants and the daily "*sellerwallahs*" who came to her house.

Sheila laughed, "Do you mean you are not used to the home service of the milkman, the fruit and vegetable sellers, and the butcher and baker? They do this to make our lives easier. We can take a taxi or our own cars, of course, but it would take the whole day because their places of business are not all in one area. Why don't you come over tomorrow and watch me interact with the *wallahs*."

Then, as was invariably the case these days, the conversation turned political. Kulwant said, "I hear Lord Mountbatten tried to persuade the leaders of the Indian National Congress and the Muslim League to settle for a united India, but Jinnah wants a land for his people. I can't see why. Sikhs, Hindus, Buddhists, Muslims, Christians, Jews, and Parsis, all want the same thing. We want independence."

"Britain wants that, too," said Steven.

"Jinnah was for a united India at one time," explained Hari. "Remember when Lord Wavell proposed a Federation of the Hindu and Muslim majority provinces? Jinnah accepted that back then. Wavell even suggested an interim government with a majority Congress representation. But Nehru and Gandhiji refused."

"Nehru and Gandhi are like two of the three monkeys, Mizaru, Kikazaru, and Iwazaru," mused

22

Steven shaking his head. "They don't see or hear that Jinnah now has the backing of seventy million Indian Muslims. The leaders should all work together."

"Which part of India will be the new country?" asked Sheila. "We have Hindus and Muslims in all areas."

"Jinnah wants Punjab, Sind, Kashmir, the North West, and Bengal for his new country," Hari replied.

***

Lahore, August 1, 1947

George Chambers, Murad's friend at the bank, walked into Murad's office after a quick knock. "Have you heard the news?"

"Which news?" asked Murad, "there is so much going on."

"Britain has given up on Viceroy Mountbatten. It now wants a divided India. Jinnah has even decided on a name for 'his' country. PAKISTAN. Pak means *pure* in Urdu. Jinnah feels he is performing an ethnic cleanse!" George grimaced. "Britain has sent a total unknown, who has never set foot in India before, to decide on the lines of demarcation between the two countries. His name is Cyril Radcliffe."

That evening, over cocktails, at Murad and Amber's house, Eric revealed that Cyril Radcliffe had actually informed the leaders of his decision to create a Pakistan with two unconnected enclaves. West Punjab would go to the Muslims and East Punjab to India. West Bengal would go to India and East Bengal to Pakistan. There would be a West Pakistan and an East Pakistan and India would stand as a wall between the two.

"What about the Princely States?" Ambika asked.

"They will be free to align themselves with either nation," Sayed said.

"You know, I never understood why India has so many independent kingdoms with ruling princes," Eric said. "How did that come about?"

"These states were areas ruled by a king, but they were never annexed by the British. The British cut a deal with them. The states became subject to subsidiary alliances in return for becoming members of the Commonwealth," Murad explained. "Their area was protected by the Company. In return, the princes paid the British East India Company for the protection."

"Ah, I had no idea," said Eric.

"Lahore, which side will Lahore be in?" Najma asked.

Murad said, "We don't know for sure, but in all probability, it will go to Pakistan."

"This is all gossip and hearsay. When will this be announced to the nation?" Ambika asked.

Eric shook his head. No one had an answer to that.

***

August 9, 1947

"Good evening. This is Saif Khan, Radio Lahore. Viceroy Lord Mountbatten has announced that Britain will transfer its power to the two brave nations of India and Pakistan at midnight this August 15th. Mr. Radcliffe has turned in his recommendations for the partition. The new boundaries will be announced on August 14, 1947."

"What the...?" Murad muttered. "They've moved the date up by a year and they are going to announce the actual boundaries one day before independence? How many people will find themselves suddenly on the wrong side of the divide? Amber, you and the children must leave right away."

Soon after this news was heard, the Muslims set fire to the largest Hindu-Sikh trading center, Shah-Almi. From a distance, it looked as if all of Lahore was burning. The situation was quickly becoming chaotic.

It was arranged that Amber and the children would leave first to stay with Murad's parents in Shimla. Four armed Baluchi guards would escort them. Murad would join them in a few days.

"We don't want to leave without you, Amber, Neil, and Nina protested.

"Don't worry, I'll be safe," Murad reassured. "I have to finish some work before I leave. I know the chief of police. He will help if necessary."

Murad handed Sayed the keys and the papers to his house. "We want you to have it. You have always wanted your parents to live close to you. It will make us happy to know that they are living here."

There was a tearful goodbye from Mahnoor whose son had insisted on taking her with him. He did not want her to go with Amber to 'another' country.

"*Ammi*, my books and all the beautiful figurines I have collected won't fit in this suitcase," Nina cried. Amber gave her a hug.

"Give them to Ayesha, she will take good care of them." Ayesha was Najma and Sayed's daughter, and Nina's best friend. "Give her all your games and toys. That will also help her from missing you too much."

Nina happily complied.

Neil was wise. He wanted to take his tennis racket with him, but he packed only a few important books and his clothes. He would have to leave everything behind when he went to Cambridge, anyway.

Amber had already taken all her jewelry from the bank safety deposit box. She had packed their important papers. She gave most of her clothes to Mahnoor. The packing was swift, as Murad had given her enough warning. Amber did not have the heart to leave Ambika's painting of her children so she packed it in her luggage.

Najma came over to visit. She brought her a *hijab*. "Wear this headgear. It will avoid suspicions," she advised. She warned Amber to be very careful. She reported that a train had just arrived from Amritsar. All the passengers were dead.

Murad had planned their journey carefully. He did not want to raise any suspicions. He knew it was possible that some Muslims could mob their car and kill his family before they left. He sent Amber and the children with the guards to the train station. They reached the station before the 6 p.m. curfew. A saloon car had been reserved for them. The guards would accompany the family in this car.

Amber felt safe as the guards from Baluchistan were tall, strong men. The train was not due to leave till 7:35 p.m. The train did not arrive on time, but the saloon car was waiting by itself at the rail yard. Amber asked a station supervisor if this was their saloon car. It was, she was told. She asked a guard if it would be safer to wait in the car instead of standing exposed on the platform. But he warned her that that might be dangerous.

"No one comes right to the main platform to openly riot," the guard explained. "But murders have been known to take place when someone is sitting in the rail yard."

They continued to wait. The guard was right. A few minutes later they saw two men with knives circling furtively around the car! Their train arrived at 9 p.m. The saloon car was quickly hitched to it, and they all got in and locked the door. Nobody slept. The train stopped at a signal, and they held their breaths. Outside they heard shouts and cries. Neil peeked out of the window.

"Armed men are running towards our train," he whispered.

Everyone was still. But then the train lurched and started, and they left the rioters behind. They talked in whispers. The atmosphere remained tense.

One of the Baluchi guards told a story about a time when his troop was stationed near a Pashtoon tribal village. The leader invited them for dinner.

"They served delicious food and offered a form of cannabis for us to smoke. We apologized for not partaking of this as we were on duty. But the tribals smoked. After dinner the leader of the tribe ordered two of his men to dance to music. As they danced, the leader joined them. He swung his sword back and forth swaying with the dancers. Then all of a sudden, he sliced one of the dancer's head off. The headless dancer continued to dance! I have never forgotten that," the guard shared softly.

Everyone gasped and then lapsed into silence till they reached Kalka. Finally they could breathe again with relief.

From Kalka, they took the toy train up to Shimla. People gave it that name because it looked like a large toy train and ran very, very, slowly. Neil jumped out of the moving train to lay a two *paise* coin on the rail track and stood back to watch the train run over the coin. He easily jumped back into the train, brandishing the expanded coin. "Look, I placed a two *paise* coin on the track. Now I have two *annas,* four times the value!"

Amber shook her head at him. But she wasn't worried that he would be left behind. Neil could run much faster than the train.

They finally reached Shimla. Murad's father was waiting at the station. The guards made the return journey to Lahore immediately. They promised Amber they would inform Murad of his family's safe arrival in Shimla.

***

Shimla 1947

Shimla was not Lahore, which was often nicknamed the 'Paris of India' because of its architecture, culture, fashion, and artists. Nevertheless, it was beautiful. Neil and Nina adjusted to their grandparent's house very quickly. They had visited Shimla many times before. The little hill town faced the largest mountain chain, the Himalayas, the glacial wall dividing India from Tibet and China. The view outside their grandparents' home was that of stark mountains, but the lower slopes were partially green with mountain fern.

Neil and Nina enjoyed walking to the Mall, the main road, with its octagonal bandstand, its teashops and stores, and the Christ Church Cathedral with its Tudor-styled belfry.

To Amber, Shimla had always seemed like a little piece of Britain. The houses with their immaculate gardens, the smaller cottages with their rose gardens, the esplanades, all were very British in appearance. Amber explained to Neil and Nina that because the entire government moved here to get away from the heat of New Delhi all the visiting diplomats were entertained here.

"During the summer months, Shimla was elegant and quite glamorous," she told them.

"And, very, very crowded, I remember," said Neil.

"Why are there so many *For Sale* signs on all these large homes?" Nina asked one day.

"Many of the British families have returned to Britain and left their homes to be sold by real estate agents," Amber explained to her.

One morning Murad's father took out an old cricket bat and ball and some wickets. He asked the whole family to join him in a game of cricket. For a while the seriousness of their situation was forgotten.

The next day they went for a walk to the Mall. A poor, stooped, man wearing spectacles was walking slowly up the hill carrying a bag of groceries when a mean, monkey took a swing at him and ran away with his glasses.

"Oh look," Nina said, "the monkey is teasing the old man. He won't return his glasses to him!"

29

The man yelled at the monkey to return his glasses, but the monkey just waved the glasses at him. Only after the man threw a banana to him did the monkey return the glasses!

"You have to watch out for the monkeys," Amber warned. "Shimla has many such monkeys. You must be careful. There is even a monkey temple on Jaku Hill. I will take you there one day."

"Oh look," Nina exclaimed pointing to a monkey that was sitting on the roof of a house. He had an unlighted cigarette in his mouth. "May we go to Jaku Hill tomorrow? I want to see this home of the monkey God, Hanuman."

"I have to help your *dadi*, grandma, with some paperwork, but maybe Ramu, the housekeeper's son can take you. He knows all the hill trails around here. He probably knows a shortcut as well. We'll ask him," Amber said.

***

Ramu was very excited at the prospect of trekking up to Jaku, which was two kilometers from *Lakkar* (wood) *Bazar*, the market that sold wooden toys and other products made of wood.

The three children left early in the morning. They each carried backpacks containing a flask of water, sandwiches and some fruit and nuts. They marched towards *Lakkar Bazar* ready to beat the heat of the sun. At the beginning of the trail, they rented walking sticks to help them climb up, and also to protect them from the monkeys.

"You know, Neil *baba*," Ramu said, "this temple came into existence during the time when our ancient text, *Ramayana* was written. Ram Chanderji's brother, Lakshmana, was injured while fighting with the demon, Ravana. A priest told them that the *sanjeevani booti,* a special herb from the Himalayan Mountains, would cure him. Lord Hanuman was sent out to find this herb. When he reached the Himalayas, he couldn't figure out which herb was the right one, so he dug up the whole mountain and flew back to Lakshmanji."

"What does that have to do with Jaku?" Neil inquired.

"Well, after Lakshmanji was healed, Hanumanji went back to replace the mountain where it was before. On the way he rested on Jaku Hill. The top of the hill became flattened due to Hanumanji's weight!" Ramu laughed. "This temple was built then."

"Do the monkeys at Jaku try to snatch people's food?" Nina asked a little worried. "Maybe we should eat our sandwiches before we reach there."

"Good idea," said Neil. "Let's take a break for a bit. Ramu, we can eat our sandwiches here."

They sat at a beautiful grassy spot to rest while they munched happily on their delicious, tomato, cheese, and *chutney* sandwiches.

The trail was steep, but the beautiful deodar trees shaded the path. The trio stopped at a few resting spots to drink water. They had filled their pockets with nuts and munched them as they walked. They were exhausted by the time they reached the top. Jaku temple was on Shimla's highest peak. The view of the city down below was spectacular. The temple was beautiful and clean inside and surrounded by greenery outside. The trek had definitely been worth it.

"Watch out for those rascal monkeys," Ramu warned.

A row of monkeys sat on a nearby wall, eyeing the visitors greedily, anticipating what they would have for lunch that day. Troops of the monkeys were in the temple enjoying the treats that the pilgrims had brought to be placed in the temple.

The trio wandered around the temple grounds for a while and then made their trek back. It was cooler now and walking downhill was a lot easier. They returned the sticks at the bottom of the hill and realized they had not needed them for walking so much as to protect themselves from the assault of one of the monkeys. Those dry-nosed, haplorhine primates were not the cute and cuddly variety.

"We must tell Papa about our trip. It was so much fun. He might want to go too," exclaimed Nina.

***

Lahore, August 1947

On August 13, 1947, Murad prepared for his departure. His friend in the Criminal Investigation Department (C.I.D) told him he should not wait any longer. The friend would lend him his staff car, which would provide a measure of safety. On the morning of the thirteenth, Murad handed his own car keys to his loyal driver, Rahim. "Keep these. You are the one who took care of this car."

Rahim burst into tears. "*Sahib*, I will keep it for you. I know you will return after all this is over. I will wait."

Murad shook his head sadly and gave Rahim a hug. He gave him an extra month's pay, and some cash for each of his three children. Then he waited for the staff car to arrive. In the car two tall, muscular, Baluchi guards accompanied the driver. His friend's car followed closely behind. His friend got out to give him a final hug. "I will miss you," they both said simultaneously.

The driver took Murad's luggage to the car, and Murad got into the front seat with the driver. The two guards sat behind. The driver stopped once for food and a little rest. Murad thought they would stay at a rest house he had stayed at frequently. When they reached the rest house, however, the *chowkidar,* security guard, warned them against this. He said the *goondas* and *thugs* came out at night to see if there were any people they could rob and kill. He told them it would be better if they spent the night hidden in the nearby jungle.

The driver drove into the jungle to park. Murad and the driver slept in the car. The guards slept outside on two blankets with a sheet to cover them. The next morning the driver was unable to start the car. Murad and the guards pushed the car a little distance, but it did not start. At that moment Murad spotted a stationary truck.

"Let's check if there is anyone in there," decided Murad. They walked to the truck. A guard peered in and glanced back somberly at the others.

"The truck is packed with corpses," he said.

They all turned around to return to their car when they heard an explosion. Their car was in flames. Someone had thrown an explosive at the car thinking that it was occupied.

"*Hai tare ki*...Now what can we do?" asked the driver.

Shimla, August 14, 1947
Murad's parents sat listening to the news on BBC. "This is BBC World News. On this day, August 14, Pakistan has announced its independence from the British. Liaquat Ali Khan has been appointed the first prime minister of Pakistan."

"I thought the independence of India and Pakistan was going to be announced, simultaneously, on the 15th," Murad's father murmured. "And where is Murad?" He shook his head, worried.

Amber booked a call to a close friend, Howard Skinner, in Lahore, to check if he knew what had happened. When her call went though there was a lot of static. She heard Howard's crackling voice. "Amber? Is everything okay?" he asked anxiously. "Are you all safe?"

"The children and I are fine, but we haven't heard from Murad. He hasn't come back," Amber replied.

"He just left yesterday. Don't worry he should be with you soon."

***

On August 15, 1947, at midnight, India declared independence. Jawaharlal Nehru was appointed India's first prime minister. Amber heard his speech on the radio.

*"Long years ago, we made a **tryst with destiny**, and now the time comes when we shall redeem our pledge, not wholly or in full measure, but very substantially. At the stroke of the midnight hour, when the world sleeps, India will awake to life and freedom. A moment comes, which comes but rarely in history, when we step out from the old to the new, when an age*

ends, and when the soul of a nation, long suppressed, finds utterance…" his speech went on but all Amber could think of was Murad's safety.

Howard Skinner called her on the August 16. "Amber, the staff car, that Murad was in, caught fire. Murad sent the guards and the driver back to Lahore. He hitched a ride from a goods trucker. I believe he is safe. I will keep in touch when I find out more about his whereabouts."

Amber prayed that Murad would be home soon.

About five days later, Howard Skinner, himself, arrived at the house. He looked grave. Amber offered him tea. He sat down. "The C.I.D sent some of their officers to assist in Murad's search. But when they reached the area, they did not find him. They found an overturned truck. It must have gone up in flames immediately because all they found was charred debris. We believe Murad was in that truck," Howard said hesitantly.

Amber felt her body go still with instant rejection. "This has to be a mistake. Murad can't be...he's still alive." Her voice broke emotionally. "I would know if he were dead."

"They found the burnt, overturned, truck on the same route the goods trucker was taking Murad on," Howard said sadly.

"I can't believe it. It can't be true," she bit out forcefully. "We'll make some more inquiries from here. They found a burnt truck. How can we know Murad was in that truck? Even if he was, he might have been thrown out before the truck exploded. He could be lying injured somewhere, for heaven's sake," she protested.

"If he was," Howard replied, "he would have tried to contact us somehow, or we would have found his body, no matter where he was, by now."

Murad's parents walked into the room just then and Howard repeated the news.

Murad's father nodded. "This is what I was afraid of."

Murad's mother let out a cry and collapsed on the floor.

"It's not true, Papa. It's not true. It can't be true." Amber shook uncontrollably now as her father-in-law went to tend to his wife. Tears cascaded down her cheeks.

"I spoke to him a few days ago. He told me how much he loved us and couldn't wait to be with his family again. Papa, you can make some inquiries on the Indian side, can't you? Maybe he crossed the border and is not near a phone service."

Murad's father nodded. "I will check with the border authorities. I know some people there. They may be able to help."

Howard sat down next to Amber on the sofa where she now sat, rocking back and forth and shivering. He put his arm around her shoulders. "I know this is a very difficult time for you, Amber. It is for me too. I met Murad at his bank a day before he planned to leave Lahore. I had some work there. He was a family man, devoted to all of you. He told me how proud he was of Neil, how much he admired your creativity and talent, and how Nina had inherited your creative genes. How she loves to paint and sing.

"He loved you all. He was happy that he would be seeing you soon. He told me that he had transferred all the family savings to the Shimla branch. Since his bank is British owned, no assets were frozen. I know he will want you to have access to the funds when you need," Howard said gently.

Murad was real. He was around. He would be back, thought Amber. "Thank you, Howard. You have gone out of your way to be helpful. But, my heart tells me that he is still alive. I feel this deeply," Amber said.

Later, she explained to Neil and Nina in a calm voice that their father was missing and efforts were being made to find him. Murad's parents called his sister, Mona, with the news. She wanted to come to Shimla right away to be with them, but her father told her it was not safe for her to travel. He told her to stay with her family. They had a prayer ceremony for Murad.

Amber was glad that no one wore white, which was the Hindu custom for mourning. There was no body, and no cremation. How could Murad be dead? Amber bowed her head and prayed for his fast and safe return.

The priest prayed for his safety. He also prayed for his soul to be at peace.

Amber was relieved that the prayer did not include the word *death*.

Howard stayed back for the ceremony. After the prayers, he came over to her. He held her hands and told her she could always call on him for any help. He was returning to England next month. "Amber, let me take Neil with me."

Amber shook her head.

"Hear me out, Amber. I want to do this for Murad. He was so proud when he heard that Neil got admission at Cambridge. I know you think you may not be able to finance Neil's education, but I believe all colleges in England have scholarships for bright students. He may not get one at the college where he has admission, but I am sure I can find one for him at another college. Please let me try. If it doesn't work out, I want at least to show him London, where his father went to school. I want to do this for Murad and Neil."

Amber realized that this was not just a favor on Howard's part. It was the evidence of a long and close friendship. India was in turmoil right now. And so was she. Neil would be better off in England. She thanked Howard gratefully. She asked him to tell her when he was going to leave, and she would arrange for Neil's passport and plane ticket.

"Let me buy both the tickets and you can pay me for Neil's," Howard suggested. Amber agreed.

Every day, she waited for news. Murad's father had contacted the border authorities to check for any knowledge of Murad's presence in the area. So far, there had been no positive news.

Neil left with Howard. He wrote to her after he reached England. Amber knew he worried about his father. Howard and his wife were taking care of him. Howard's son, George, and Neil, were close friends, too.

Amber walked around the house listlessly. She was happy when Neil called one day to say he had been granted a scholarship at a college in Oxford. It was closer to London. Howard could stay in more frequent touch with him.

In September, Amber's father-in-law reminded her that schools had reopened in July and that she needed to enroll Nina. "Speak to the Mother Superior at Loreto Convent. Tell her about your circumstances. I am sure she will be sympathetic to enrolling Nina even though she is a few months late."

The next day, Amber and Nina walked up to Loreto Convent. It was a warm grey and red structure with sprawling green grassy area in the center. The colorful flowers welcomed each visitor. Amber liked the school. Mother Superior was in her office. Amber introduced herself and Nina. She had brought all of Nina's previous transcripts, which were impressive.

Mother Superior agreed to enroll Nina. "Many of the British students enrolled at the school have left. Some of the teachers have gone too. I can enroll Nina, immediately, and if you know of any teachers looking for a job, please refer them to me."

Impulsively, Amber told her about her teaching degree and her interest in working at this school. She was going crazy at home, worried about Murad.

"Have you taught before?" asked Mother Superior.

"No, but I coached my own children, and I taught our housekeeper's son."

Mother Superior smiled. "All right, I'll hire you, but only on a trial basis. I need a second standard teacher. Come in tomorrow when you bring Nina. Bring in your transcripts. Here are some forms that you'll need to fill out."

As they walked back home, Amber thought of her parents and her sister, Aparna. She hoped they had left Bhakkar when she had told them to. How were they doing? She wondered. Her aunt, Vimla, did not have much information. She had told Amber that her father's younger brother, Raj, was looking out for them hoping to see them on a train coming from Pakistan. Amber hoped they were safe. These were such uncertain times.

Bhakkar, August 1947
A crowd led by the village *chowdary,* the headman, had gathered outside Mr. Vij's house. The headman was trying to pacify the crowd.
"The partition will not affect us in this village. We are Hindus, Sikhs, and Muslims, but we are all farmers. We are brothers, bound together by our work. Our enemies are the greedy merchants that set the wholesale prices."
Amber's father, Vikram Vij, walked out towards the crowd. The village head stepped forward.
"*Vakil sahib,* you are a big man, a lawyer. Please help us. It is peaceful here, but we hear news that there is trouble in the cities. There have been killings. Hindus and Sikhs are killing Muslims, and Muslims are killing Sikhs and Hindus. Women are being raped and harmed. Many young girls have jumped into wells and lakes to drown rather than face their terrible fate. The *Angrezi sarkar* is not doing anything. Should we worry? Do you think there may be an uprising here?"
"The British government has a lot on its hands. But I don't think anyone will create an uprising in our own village," replied Mr. Vij thoughtfully. "However, we must stay alert for outsiders who may try to make trouble. Stay vigilant."

The villagers nodded thoughtfully and left. Vikram Vij's optimism proved to be ill founded. Just three weeks later, one of Vikram Vij's clients, whose case he had fought and won, came to inform him of a major threat from a nearby village. They had to evacuate or face a threat to their lives. Amber's father stood outside his house. He had to leave his home and this city where he was born and had worked, married, and raised a family. This town had been good to him. He had built a thriving practice as a criminal attorney. He had represented, *pro bono*, many of the poor villagers who had been wrongly accused of stealing or even murder.

Bhakkar was dry, treeless, and sandy, but looking across at the canal, which was the overflow water from the Indus River, he could see his date and mango groves flourishing. His dates were delicious, and he exported them all the way to Kabul.

Vikram Vij enjoyed his law practice, but he was also a farmer at heart, a man who had worked on the land himself. Though he employed several workers, he took a great interest in his crops. Amber's father did not want to leave all this. There were two choices; stay here and convert to Islam, or remain a Hindu but move to an unfamiliar place in newly partitioned India. Neither option appealed to him but he preferred the latter. In the end there was only one choice. He went into the house to talk to his wife. He explained that they would have to travel lightly.

"Bury any precious items in the ground. When all this is over, and we return, we can dig them out again," he told his wife. He told her he had dug a hole under the clay oven. "Bring all your jewelry and any gold coins that you have accumulated," he advised. "We'll cover the hole with mud and replace the oven over the hole."

His wife followed his instructions.

Several relatives had arrived from nearby villages where there had been problems. They, along with the household help, would accompany Aparna and Amber's families. Mr. Vij had planned an escape route to his daughter's house.

It was a dark, moonless, night when Vikram Vij, along with twenty-five others, escaped to his oldest daughter, Sarla's, house. The house was two miles away but they took a short cut to avoid all the winding streets. They leaped from rooftop to rooftop over makeshift bridges, unnoticed by anyone on the streets below. There was no electricity to worry about.

Sarla's family home had sixty suites of rooms where she and her 'joint' family lived. The iron alloy of the front door made it impenetrable when locked. However, an enemy could jump in through the open courtyard in the center of the house. The family was prepared for that. They had large pots of hot oil and water ready to pour over anyone who tried to harm the family.

The escape party reached Sarla's house safely. Sarla's husband and his entire family welcomed them joyfully. Each member was accommodated. It had been a hot day but the night was cool. Everyone sat around a fire, not sleeping. They had to stay vigilant. The large pots of boiling water and oil were ready, just in case. But they seemed to be safe. Some fell asleep on their cots. At 4 a.m. there was a soft thud.

"Who is it?" called out Sarla's husband. "Show yourself."

The intruder's face was covered; only his eyes could be seen. "You are all infidels, unfaithful to Allah!" he yelled in a raspy voice. "I have a hundred people with me. All of you will be gone before dawn!"

Amber's father was armed by now. He came from behind and grabbed the intruder by the neck with one arm and pulled his arms behind his back with the other.

"We are fully armed in this *haveli*," Mr. Vij shouted. "We have swords, *kirpans*, sharp knives, and hot oil. We will disarm you."

Another man from the enemy camp jumped in. But this time, the family members were prepared and grabbed him before he had a chance to make his move. Someone tore the cloth away from his mouth.

Mr. Vij stared at the man's face in astonishment. "Mohammad Ali, you? Just last month you came begging me to save you. I won your case for you. And you think *we* are unfaithful. Aren't you ashamed of yourselves? We all lived like family for years, and now *we* have become the infidels? You may have a hundred people, but we are several, and we have courage and strength on our side. Go back out and tell your people. We don't want to fight you, but we will," Mr. Vij said firmly.

The two men had the grace to look ashamed. They weren't passionate about this cause. Even though their group had incited them, they realized the truth of Vikram Vij's words. The men ran back to their companions. No one from that group threatened the household again, but everyone knew it was only a

43

matter of time before some other village group would take it upon themselves to invade their privacy and harm the family. They had to make other plans.

"We will have to leave soon," said one of the women. "I heard today that houses are being burned down. Also, we have nearly run out of all our food."

"True, we will have to leave for India. People have stopped thinking and are just following the mob," another family member agreed.

"Ever since Pakistan announced its independence last week and hoisted the green flag, the people here have gone crazy," said another, shaking his head sadly.

"*Kali Yuga*, the age of downfall, is here!" exclaimed a family member. "We must leave."

***

Good fortune came their way some weeks later when a convoy of army trucks stopped by. They told them that they were there to guide them safely to the train station if they wished to cross the border into India. The family agreed. They took only what little they could carry in their hands. Most of them just walked out of the house with what they were wearing and little more.

After the announcement of the independence, one-third of the *British Indian Army* changed its name to the *Pakistan Army* with the motto: *Faith, Piety, and Fight in the path of God.* Two thirds were called the *First Indian National Army* with their motto: *Service before self.* Both armies wanted the safety of the citizens.

***

The convoys drove the family straight to the train station where a freight train was waiting. The four front compartments were for passengers, and the freight cabins were empty and without seats so many people could pack in. At the back were four open containers. Many squeezed themselves in those. They thought, sitting in this container without a roof would be better than sitting in a dark, windowless, freight compartment. The doors to these windowless cars could be left open, but they were still uncomfortable. There were no toilets.

Mr. Vij, with most of his family members, found accommodations in the passenger compartments. They wondered what was in store for them on the other side of the border. The journey of eighteen hours proved exhausting and frightening. Even though there were military guards, at every stop, to provide a measure of safety for the passengers, the danger of rioters overpowering the guards was always there.

At one stop, they heard horses and shouts, but they quickly shut the windows and locked their compartment doors. They heard the people in the goods compartments, slide the doors shut with a loud bang. Everyone prayed for the safety of the people in the open compartments.

Most of the passengers were hungry and tired. Amber's mother shared a large sack of almonds with the other passengers from time to time. At one station, there was water service, and everyone drank thirstily.

Finally, they reached Jalandhar, India. Everyone disembarked, and looked around, disoriented. Someone yelled. The last two open compartments held a pile of corpses. They had been killed in spite of the guards. Several of the women were missing. There was no doubt the perpetrators of these killings had carried them away.

"Those butchers! And God alone knows what they have done to our women," someone exclaimed.

"*Rab Rakha,*" said a bearded Sikh man, looking upwards. "May God protect their souls."

The police said they would try to determine the identities of the dead, but most of the passengers knew it was futile. No one had the time for those not living. There was too much to do.

***

Refugee Camp Jalandhar, 1947

From the train station, Aparna, Amber's seventeen-year-old sister, and the rest of her family from Bhakkar, were guided to the refugee camp and checked in. The camp was a city of tents. Aparna had never seen so many. Her family was allotted a small tent. The rest of the families lived in nearby tents.

Inside, the tent was bare except for a *duree* or thin carpet. The *charpais* or cots would be delivered later. On one side lay a large clay pot with a narrow neck, a *surahi*, filled with water. A metal drinking cup covered the opening. Aparna was so tired, she could have slept anywhere.

Aparna's father went to investigate the facilities. He returned an hour later.

"There are women's toilets on that end," he informed his wife, pointing to the right end. Close by is the area where women can take a bath. On the left side are clay ovens where we can cook our own food. We will be given rationed supplies later, but for the next week, we will be provided with milk and cooked food."

"Did you find out if there are any schools, nearby, for Aparna?" his wife asked.

"Yes, there is one right here in the camp. She can start right away."

"But I don't have any clothes," Aparna protested. "I can't wear these." She gestured to her soiled and wrinkled apparel.

Aparna's father nodded understandingly. "There is a clothing supply facility just ten tents down. Free clothing is available. Go to check if you can find something that fits."

From complete chaos, life took on a flow. Vikram Vij went to the reemployment and rehabilitation tent every day to see if he could get a job. Mrs. Vij made friends with people in the neighboring tents. She joined the other women at the ovens, to cook the meals, or go with them to the bathing area where she bathed and washed the family's clothes. Aparna went to school every morning. Her clothes and shoes were ill fitting, but she was happy to be alive. Everyone at the camp faced the same situation. She knew some of the girls from her village already, and she made many new friends as well.

She liked the atmosphere at the refugee camp. The residents of the camp were like a huge family. Despite the inconveniences, there was also new hope.

"Aparna, they are going to show a Donald Duck movie tonight. Do you want to come with us?" a new friend called out to her one evening.

Large cloth screens, allowing for two-way projection, showed Disney cartoons, featuring Mickey Mouse and Donald Duck. Thousands came out to watch them. Aparna loved to watch these cartoons. The characters were so sweet and funny. For a few hours, gales of laughter came from the movie-watching audience. During this time, the homeless and even the wounded, laughed. For a few hours, they forgot their experiences of fear, hurt, loss, and misery. For those few hours they enjoyed the fun and simplicity of the cartoons.

Every morning the refugees awakened to Hindu or Sikh religious chants over loudspeakers. People went about their way chanting to themselves. There was a sense of optimism. The need to move on with life brought people closer to each other.

One day, as Aparna walked home after school with her classmates, she noticed a large, shady tree. "Let's sit there for half an hour. It is so hot. I don't think our parents will worry too much if we are a little late returning." Her friends agreed and they all settled down under the tree to make idle conversation.

"Our teacher, Mrs. Grewal, is really patient. I liked the way she explained that geometry problem so well," Aparna said.

"Yes," her friend replied.

"This camp is nice. We are all like one large family," another girl observed.

"We refugees are unlike the others who live in this city, and things are certainly different from the way we lived in our own homes."

"That's true," agreed another. "We have had to break away from old traditions and customs because, along with our parents, we all want to move forward with our lives. We don't have the old social differences. Everyone helps one another."

"My father took my mother to the grocery market, the *mandi*, on his bicycle. My mother proudly sat on the handlebars! They would not have done that two months ago. They looked so funny but also sweet. I think they have become closer."

"Yes," Aparna giggled. "My parents would never have sat on the same *charpai*, a bed, in front of others. Now they do it all the time. There is not enough space."

Another spoke out, "This lack of space can be very embarrassing."

"What do you mean?"

"Well, last night, my father came home late from a job. My mother heated him some food. I was lying at one end of the tent with my eyes closed. After he finished his dinner, my dad told my mother he was very tired. Would she massage his shoulders and his feet? I peeked. My mother was massaging his shoulders when he pulled her on top of him."

Someone groaned. "Stop, please."

But the girl continued to tell her story. "I heard my mother protesting, telling him to stop, saying that I was right there. But my dad told her not to worry because 'I was sleeping' and I wouldn't know. They whispered so loudly and obliviously thought I couldn't hear! I kept my eyes shut, but I kept hearing heavy breathing, and weird sounds."

Someone interrupted her at this point. "Shut up. You are disgusting. Talking about your parents that way. They must at least be in their fifties, for God's sake."

"You know what I've been feeling homesick for?" Aparna exclaimed changing an uncomfortable subject. "I miss all our great celebrations, our festivals, watching the story of Ram Chanderji enacted, the burning of the demon, Ravana, during *Dusshera*, and lighting the lamps during *Diwali*, although I absolutely don't miss the fireworks!"

"I think we have heard the sounds of enough explosions," another agreed fervently.

"You know what I miss? I miss playing outside our home, around the sand dunes on full moon nights. It was so beautiful," remembered another.

"Yes, all those traditions have a symbolic importance," another reminded them. "Without them, life slips away from us, the way sand blows away in a windstorm. We have no sense of time passing if we don't notice the first monsoon shower, the first sign of winter, open fires on the coldest winter day, or the first flowers in spring."

Just then two little boys ran towards the group, waving a toy in the hands. "Look what Mohan *Cha Cha*, gave us? An aeroplane! We are flying planes."

Mohan *Cha Cha* or Mohan Uncle, as he was fondly called, was a carpenter from Sialkot. During the day he worked as a carpenter for a store in the city but when he returned to the camp, he rummaged through the trash and found items to recycle into imaginative toys for the children.

"Let's go visit Mohan *Cha Cha,*" cried one of Aparna's friends. "Let's see what new toys he has made. Maybe we can help him." They stopped off at their tents to tell their mothers where they were all going.

Mohan *Cha Cha* showed them airplanes he had made of wire, pieces of metal, and wood. He displayed his toys proudly to the crowd that had gathered around him. "These are aeroplanes. Have any of you flown before?" The children shook their heads, wide-eyed.

"When you grow up, you will. You are now in *Azad*, independent India. You are survivors. Remember that," he told them. "Look at this one. It is a *Douglas DC-3* and this is a *Vultee Vengeance*. They were both designed in *Amrika*. It is a great country. This is a *Hawker Hurricane*. This is the *Supermarine Spitfire*. And this one is the *Westland Lysander*. These were made in *Vilayat*, England. One day all of you will fly all over the world. You will be able to fly around the world in one day!" he concluded in the voice of a prophet.

"*Cha Cha* have you ever flown in an aeroplane?" a child asked him in awe.

"Many, many times," *Cha Cha* said, grinning wickedly. "Right here," he said pointing to his head.

"*Cha Cha* may we help you make some toys?" Aparna's friend asked.

"Sure, sit right here. I'll show you what to do."

Other refugees sometimes asked Mohan *Cha Cha* why he spent so much time making toys and then gave them away. He could easily have put a price tag on his beautiful creations.

"These are difficult times," the carpenter told them, "and these little children have been traumatized enough. Their happiness brings meaning to my life."

Life in the refugee camp was not bad but it was not great. There was a head lice infestation. All the women cut their hair. Where the infestations got worse, they shaved their heads. There was a spread of cholera, dysentery, and hepatitis. Aparna's mother was dehydrated, and if it weren't for Dr. Luthra and his son, Dev, who came to help, she would have died from dysentery. Dr. Luthra was a refugee in the same camp, but now he worked as the camp doctor and had become a good friend of Aparna's father.

Dev, was not a doctor. He was in school with her, but he helped his father on his rounds. Aparna knew him and his sister, Monica. She also knew that Dev was attracted to her from the long, hooded looks, he turned on her. Until now she had ignored him.

After attending to her mother, Dr. Luthra walked out with her father. He told him that his wife would be fine and not to worry.

"Did you hear that Pakistan invaded, independent Kashmir on October 22 but the Indian army has helped to defeat them?" he questioned Aparna's father.

Mr. Vij nodded.

***

The newspapers had full-page stories of the Kashmir situation. The British had agreed that the Maharaja of Kashmir could rule his state independently because the Hindu Maharaja, Hari Singh, wanted a neutral Kashmir. But both India and Pakistan had their eyes on it. Jinnah wanted it because it was predominantly Muslim and Nehru wanted it because it was his beautiful birthplace. His family was Kashmiri Brahmin

On October 22, 1947 Pakistani tribal *pathans* invaded Kashmir. They knew the hilly area well. When they reached Poonch, they gathered the support of the locals and advanced towards Srinagar. India secretly sent arms and ammunition to the Kashmiri Armed Forces. Brigadier Rajinder Singh Jamwal stemmed the tribal advance for two days but he was wounded and the tribals put up a flag for *Azad Kashmir*. They had freed that portion of Kashmir from the evils of the Maharaja and India. Violence broke out.

The Kashmiri Hindu maharaja appealed to the Indian Government for help. On October 26, Lord Mountbatten sent V.P. Menon to Jammu to get the Maharaja to sign an instrument of succession to India. This allowed the Indian Army to intervene and oust the *pathans*. Sardar Patel requisitioned all the planes owned by private airlines, and within hours, over a hundred aircraft were deployed and India took over Kashmir via an air strike and the Pakistani tribals were defeated.

"Yes," said Vikram Vij. "I heard Sheikh Abdullah has been placed in charge, replacing the Maharaja. However the areas of Gilgit and Baltisthan, continue to be called *Azad* Kashmir, Free Kashmir. That area has its own leaders and government but they are under the Federation of Pakistan," said Mr. Vij shaking his head.

"Yes," sighed Dr. Luthra. "I wonder when all the fighting will end?"

***

While the two fathers were talking, Dev turned to Aparna. "Don't worry, your mother will be all right. My father has given her a shot. She will be fine. I have seen other patients like her get well."

She asked curiously, "Are you planning to be a doctor, too?"

"Not a chance. I am going to be an air force pilot. I have always wanted to fly. Have you ever flown in a plane?"

This was the second time someone had asked her this question today. Aparna shook her head. "No, I don't know if planes are safe."

53

Dev grinned. "Once you have been on a plane, you won't want to use any other transport. You know how long it takes to go to Europe by ship? Almost two weeks. You know how long it takes to go to America by sea? Several months. Just hours on an aeroplane. I am ready. I promise you, when I am a pilot, I will fly you wherever you want to go."

Aparna rolled her eyes in disbelief. "Oh, please!"

Dr. Luthra and her father joined them just then. The doctor smiled at Aparna. "Your mother will be fine. There is nothing to worry about."

Aparna thanked them before they left.
Dr. Luthra and his son, Dev, visited them many times, until finally, Aparna's mother was well again. Dev made it a habit to stay and talk to Aparna while his father talked to Mr. Vij. "I'd like to see you after I am through helping my father this evening," Dev said. "We can go for a walk. I can bring my sister, Monica, along, if you like," he suggested one day.

"I don't know. People might talk," she replied.

"Haven't you noticed? People in this camp don't care about the old customs and traditions anymore? Boys and girls talk freely with one another. There is no caste or class system here. No one says, 'I am rich and I am better than you who are poor.' We are all in the same boat or refugee camp. We just want to move forward."

"I don't know if my parents would approve," Aparna hesitated.

"Okay, I promise we'll be discreet," Dev said. "I'll persuade Monica to come along."

Aparna liked him. She knew Monica well, so she agreed.

Having given her promise, Aparna walked back to her tent to look in on her mother. Her father was sitting beside her mother on the cot. He had applied a cold compress to her forehead, as Dr. Luthra had suggested, keeping her cool in the triple-digit heat.

"I am glad you are feeling better," her father said to his wife. "I went to visit the Department of Rehabilitation today. I was told that even though I had a hundred acres of farmland back home; they could not replace all my land, acre for acre. Hindus and Sikhs left behind 6.7 million acres in West Punjab but here in the East only 4.6 million acres are available, and the land is not as rich as ours."

"So, how much land will we get?" her mother asked.

"We can get only four acres for now, until they rehabilitate every farmer," her father said shaking his head. "Later the Department of Rehabilitation will give us more land, but it may not be in Jalandhar. It could be in any part of Northern India. It will be difficult to manage the farms in different areas. I will have to decide what to do. But the department has agreed to give me a loan if I want to purchase farm equipment and seeds."

"So in the meantime, we have to stay at this camp?" her mother asked.

Aparna was shocked to hear what her father said next.

"Maybe for another week. I have got a job in Panipat, about 56 miles north of our capital, New Delhi. I have been appointed Chief Rations Officer. I will

55

make sure that each refugee is issued a ration card and there are sufficient basic supplies for everyone."

Aparna placed her hands over her ears. But she could still hear. She had just made new friends. She did not want to move away from them, especially Dev.

"We will get a temporary house. Later we will get our own house in exchange for the one we left behind. This may be in Faridabad, about thirty miles south, or in Gurgaon, about twenty miles southwest of New Delhi. When we get our house, I will resume my law practice again in that town," her father continued. "At this time we can't be choosers. We have to make the most of our new lives."

Oh no, Aparna thought in dismay. *Would they have to keep moving?*

She shared this news with Dev and Monica that evening when she met them. They were disappointed to hear this but Dev told her she could write to him at the camp to tell him her new address. He and his sister promised to keep in touch.

"Don't worry," Dev grinned confidently. "Our fathers are good friends. They will stay in touch. I will find you. I have to give you a ride on my plane, after all."

November, 1949 Shimla

It was the summer of nineteen forty-nine. So much had changed since India's partition from Pakistan in 1947. The world had changed.

The Communist Peoples Republic of China under Mao Tse Tung was established. Indonesia had gained independence from the Netherlands.

The American president, Harry Truman, had just announced his four-point program to help developing countries.

Pakistan had lost its leader, Mohammad Ali Jinnah to tuberculosis and heart failure.

India had had lost her beloved hero, *bapu*, Mahatma Gandhi. *Bapu* had changed the country so much. He preached non-violence, the removal of the caste system and religious bigotry. But on January 30, 1948, a Hindu extremist shot him.

India had moved forward. It had formed its own constitution after the parliamentary system of Britain. It was getting ready to become the *Republic of India*.

Nearly all the refugees from West Pakistan had been rehabilitated. Some from East Pakistan were still waiting in camps.

Amber's life had changed. She had made contact with her parents. They had left Pakistan in time and had lived in a refugee camp until her father was able to find a job. They moved to whichever city her father found temporary work. They were now living in the capital city of New Delhi where her father had acquired a house as a replacement for the one he had left behind. He had started a law practice specializing in getting refugees their rights. Amber's younger sister, Aparna, now nineteen, attended the Delhi University. She planned to go on to study law.

Amber and her daughter, Nina still lived with Murad's parents. Amber's son, Neil, was doing well at Oxford. He spent his holidays with their family friend, Howard Skinner. Amber had opened an account for Neil in her bank, which had a branch in Oxford. Neil could easily withdraw funds she deposited for him.

Nina was sixteen years old, nearly a graduate. Amber had gone on to get a Masters in Education.

Ironically, as soon as Amber had the degree in her hand, Mother Superior had promoted her to the position of Vice Principal. Mother Superior recognized her intelligence and her ability to interact with people. Now Mother Superior dealt with the administrative details. Amber dealt with the problems of parents, teachers, and students. She had been offered a small cottage on the school grounds to live in, but Amber had refused. She knew Murad's parents would break if she and Nina left. Their last thread of attachment to Murad would be torn asunder.

It was over two years since she had last heard from Murad. Last year she had heard from the Lahore police department that they had listed Murad Mehra as 'deceased.' Why would they list him that way when his body had never been recovered? The paper record of 'deceased' was a convenience for the government authorities. Their search was over. The pain and anguish of Murad's absence was gut wrenching for Amber. In her heart she continued to feel that one day he would return.

It was with a heavy heart that she walked up the hill with her daughter, Nina, towards Loreto Convent.

**

"Ma, is that cute little girl still coming to your office?" Nina asked.

"Rowena? She is. She keeps getting into trouble and her teacher sends her to me. One day, when I asked her why she misbehaved, that precocious little girl told me, it was because she liked me! She said she liked being in my room. But finally she told me that the other girls teased her because she didn't have a mother or father, which was, according to her, 'a big fat lie.' She said she did have a mother and father. Her father was a very important man who travelled a lot. I believe her mother died of cancer but Rowena told me her mother was a twinkling star in the sky. She could talk to her every night." Amber chuckled. "I don't know why, but I can't help loving that little girl."

"She looks like a little angel," commented Nina. "After you told me to watch out for her, I did keep an eye on her. But you know, Ma, I found out she actually instigates some of those arguments. She is a cutie, but there is no halo hovering over her head!"

"I did tell Rowena she may come to see me whenever she wants, but I don't want her coming to my office as a punishment. So far, she has only come once after our talk. I have spoken to her grandmother. She is the one who told me Rowena's mother died of cancer when Rowena was six years old, and her father is a hotelier who travels a lot. She said she would talk to Rowena. Her grandmother is also an acquaintance of your *dadi*, grandma," Amber shared.

When Amber reached the school, Nina walked to her classroom, to drop off her satchel, while a teacher, who wanted to discuss a problem, stopped Amber. Problem solved, Amber joined Mother Superior at the playground where the students lined up every morning for Assembly and the singing of the national anthem. It was a lovely moment when the whole school sang in unison.

The assembly always ended with Saint Francis' prayer.

Lord, make me an instrument of Your peace.
Where there is hatred, let me sow love;
Where there is injury, pardon; where there is doubt,
faith;
Where there is despair, hope; where there is darkness,
light;
Where there is sadness, joy.
O, Divine Master, grant that I may not seek to be
consoled as to console;
To be understood as to understand; to be loved as to
love;
For it is in giving that we receive; it is in pardoning that
we are pardoned;
It is in dying that we are born again to eternal life.

After the prayer, Mother Superior made announcements and then the teachers led their students back to their classes.

This prayer had always provided Amber with solace. But today, she gave in to despair, sadness, and darkness. It suddenly hit her that Murad may never come back. She didn't want to let go of her hope for Murad's safe return. But was that just wishful thinking on her part? Should she release him from her life and allow him to be at peace? She wanted answers.

Amber walked into her office and saw a new mountain of work. She had letters to write to parents, letters to be answered, reports to be read, and memos to send out. With her elbows on her desk, Amber rested her face on her hands.

Slowly she lifted her head and went to work. She worked straight through the morning. She stopped when the recess bell rang. Amber stood up and walked out to the playground.

When she reached the grounds, she saw the girls playing on monkey bars, the jungle gym, the seesaw, while some were playing tag or just standing around talking.

Amber smiled. It was such a happy scene. Suddenly she saw a little girl run towards her. "Miss Amber! Miss Amber!" she yelled and then gave her a big hug. It was the adorable Rowena. "Come see me hang from the monkey bars," she begged. "I can go from one end to the other without falling." Amber was glad to note that Rowena happy but was disturbed to see her playing alone.

Rowena demonstrated her moves as she brachiated from one end to the other. Amber clapped her hands. "That was great, Rowena. Now why don't we go join your friends?"

"I'd rather stay here and play on my own. No one wants to play with me. They think **I** fight, but that's not true. **They** fight with me." She continued to go back and forth while Amber watched.

"Come now, I have to watch the other students as well. I will introduce you to a wonderful little girl," Amber told her, holding out her hand. "You will like Sonia. She is bright and loves to have fun, but right now her little brother is in the hospital awaiting surgery. She worries about him and is very sad. Will you be a good friend to her? I know you can cheer her up."

Rowena nodded solemnly. "Yes, Miss Amber, I'll be her friend."

Sonia was a plump little girl with a round face and large brown eyes. Lively curls hung around her face. But she sat alone. She looked pensive.

"Hello Sonia, I've brought you a new friend," Amber smiled introducing Rowena.

"I know who she is. I've seen her in my class. Will you be my friend, Sonia?" Rowena asked.

Sonia nodded.

Rowena held out her hand. "Come. I'll teach you to hang on the monkey bars. It's fun."

They ran towards the monkey bars. Amber smiled.

After that Amber often saw the two girls sitting together during break or during lunch. Rowena was not sent to her office anymore.

***

Mrs. Kapoor, Rowena's grandmother, also noticed how much happier her granddaughter looked. Rowena did not fuss about her homework and completed it fast.

"*Dadi*, today I am going to draw a beautiful picture for my friend Sonia's brother. He is in the hospital. I told her she could take it to him when she visits."

"That is very thoughtful of you, *meri nunni see jaan*, my sweet little life." Her grandmother bent down to kiss her forehead and give her a hug.

"You know, Miss Amber asked me to be Sonia's friend. Sonia used to be sad because of her brother. Now she talks to me about him. Can we go see her soon? She lives in that house up on that hill."

"Of course, as long as she gets permission from her parents. I'll walk you to her house," replied her grandmother gently.

"And can we also go to visit Miss Amber? You said you knew her mother," Rowena pleaded.

"We'll see. Go draw your picture."

"I am going to draw the Himalayas. I will draw its highest peak, Mt. Everest. I will draw trees, monkeys, our school, and Sonia and me, playing. He will like that."

"I am sure he will," her grandmother said smiling at her fondly.

"*Dadi*, when is Papa, coming home again?"

Her grandmother held up the palm of her hand, "Five days."

"Oh, yippee! I miss him so much. I feel so sorry for Papa, don't you? At least you and I have each other. Papa has no one. He must be so lonely."

Rowena's grandmother shook her head. Sometimes little Rowena surprised her with her mature perspective.

***

Amber and her family were enjoying a quiet evening together. Amber and Nina were at the dining table. Nina completed her homework. Amber finished some paper work she had brought home from school. Amber's father-in-law read the evening newspaper. It was only four pages, but it contained the latest news. Her mother-in-law sat, knitting a sweater for Nina.

During this time the housekeeper came to tell them there was an elderly lady and a young girl at the front door.

Mrs. Mehra looked up. "Who are they? Bring them in."

They were surprised to see Rowena and her grandmother walking in.

"Mrs. Kapoor! This is a wonderful surprise. What brings you here?" Mrs. Mehra stepped forward, welcoming them. "We were not expecting you."

"I hope you don't mind. Rowena has been dying to visit Miss Amber, and since you and I know each other well, I thought I would bring her. It also gives me an opportunity to get to know your daughter-in-law. My granddaughter can't stop talking about her."

"Miss Amber!" little Rowena exclaimed. She ran to hug her. Amber hugged her back. She couldn't help loving this little bundle of energy.

The visitors were offered tea and snacks. Nina taught Rowena how to play *Carrom*. She pulled out the old *Carrom Board* that her parents and Neil and Nina had used. Mrs. Kapoor thanked Amber for all she had done for her granddaughter.

"Rowena does not remember her mother well. She was too young when she died. My daughter-in-law was sick for a few years before she died. She couldn't really care for her child. Nayan took care of her while he was in town. Otherwise her nanny brought her up. My son, Nayan, is a good father, but he has to take care of the family business as well. He doesn't have the time he would like to have to take care of Rowena.

"I worry about her. When I got the news that she was fighting in school, my worry for her increased. But you have helped her so much. I appreciate that. Rowena is a happier girl. Thank you."

"She needs her father's attention," Amber murmured in reply. "It would help if her father could spend more time with her."

***

"Papa!" Rowena screamed when she saw her father near the gate of their house. Nayan bent his six-foot frame to hug his daughter. His thick black hair was brushed carelessly across his forehead. His face was bold and rugged, his complexion bronzed by the exposure to the sun. His cleft deepened as he smiled at his daughter.

Strong arms encircled Rowena. The open happiness and affection brought tears to his mother's eyes as she watched them from the front door.

"How are you, my little angel?" Nayan asked his daughter picking her up and hugging her tightly. "I have missed you so much. Do you know how much I love you?" he asked clutching her closer.

"Yes, Papa, you love me more than the Universe, but I love you more," she giggled. Nayan held on to his daughter for several minutes, just breathing her in. He hated to leave her, but he had taken over his deceased father's failing hotel business and had struggled to keep it alive, and then to expand it. He had gone on to buy several failing hotels and turned them around. He seemed to have a knack. But what he really wanted was to be able to spend more time with his daughter whom he adored.

"I'm so happy to see you, Papa," Rowena cried. "Did you bring me something?"

He always did. "Let's go inside, and I'll show you."

Nayan's mother welcomed him in. He bent

down to hug her. She framed his face between her hands. "Let me look at you. You seem tired," she said shaking her head. "The hotels are doing fine. You have appointed reliable managers. It's time you slowed down a little," she admonished.

"I know *Ammi*, I know, and I promise you I will."

"Papa, show me what you brought for me." Nayan opened his briefcase and pulled out a silver foil wrapped, gift.

"It's a box," cried Rowena. "What is it?"

Nayan handed it to Rowena. She shook it. It rattled. She started to tear open the package. "It's a game! SCRABBLE," she read.

Nayan nodded. "Remember the game, *Lexiko,* we used to play together? Well, this is a newer version of the game designed by the same person. It's a brand new game from America. We can learn how to play it together.

"And I can play it with my friend, Sonia, and Miss Amber and Nina. Thank you so much, Papa," Rowena hugged her father tightly. "Will you teach me now?"

"Let your father rest and enjoy a cup of tea first," her grandmother admonished. "Why don't you sit with him and tell him about your school and your friends."

Rowena sat with her father, chatting happily. "Papa, I have a new friend. Her name is Sonia. Miss Amber asked me to be Sonia's friend. You know her brother is in the hospital, and sometimes she gets sad. But as long as I am her friend she is happy. I want you to meet her."

"Sure, you can invite her over. I would love to meet her."

"And I want you to meet Miss Amber. Her daughter's name is Nina. Nina taught me how to play *Carrom*. Miss Amber says I can visit her any time. I like her. *Dadi* took me to their house one day. If you like, I will take you to their house tomorrow." Rowena chattered on.

Nayan had two cups of tea. His mother's delicious tea always energized him. "Okay, Row, Row, I'm getting the game out. *Ammi* would you like to join us? If you join us today, we can all learn the game together"

***

The three of them sat around the game board on the carpeted floor as Nayan read the rules. "It says two to four players can play. We are three, so we are fine. The object of the game is to score more points than the other players."

He showed them a plastic square with a letter of the alphabet and a small number below. "Each letter has a different point value. So the way to score well is to play words with high scoring letter combinations. Look at this board. It is 15 cells wide and 15 cells high. The scrabble tiles fit within these cells.' Nayan emptied the cloth bag filled with tiles. He mixed them up and turned them face down.

"There are one hundred tiles. Each of us has to pick one tile. The one that gets closest to the alphabet **A** gets to begin."

Rowena pulled out **D**. Mrs. Kapoor got an **H**. Nayan got **B**. He got the first pick. He took seven tiles from the pile and placed them on his tile rack. "Now each of you gets seven tiles. The words you make, must be from this Oxford English Dictionary," Nayan informed pointing to the book. "You cannot use abbreviations or prefixes or hyphenated words and, definitely, no Hindi words like you used when we were in Delhi."

"That wasn't me! That was *Dadi.* And we can use Hindi words. What about, *avatar, bungalow, cheetah, cot, pajamas?*"

"I said as long as they are in the Oxford English dictionary Miss Clever. Shall we begin? We know the basics now. We can learn more about the game as we go along," grumbled Nayan good-naturedly.

Nayan made his first word: WHIP

Rowena counted the points, "four, four, one, and three. Daddy you have twelve points."

Nayan wrote down the points on a piece of paper and picked up four more tiles.

"I have so many vowels on my rack," Rowena wailed. "I will have to exchange some of them. No, wait. I got a word, AERIE, an eagle's nest located on a cliff. We learned about it at school."

"That was great," her grandmother praised. "You got five points, and you did not lose a turn for exchanging the tiles. You are a quick thinker."

"Okay *Ammi*, your turn," Nayan pushed.

"BOWL, three, one, four, one. I have nine points."

Rowena beamed at her grandma. "That was good, *dadi.*"

As Nayan played, he thought about how a simple game could bring so much happiness. The three played, argued, laughed, and just enjoyed each other's company.

"Papa, may I take this game to school to show Miss Amber? I am sure she does not know of this one," Rowena begged.

"Leave it at home," her grandmother advised, "you may lose it in school. Why don't I invite Miss Amber and her family for tea? We need to return their hospitality, after all. You can show it to her then. Sonia might like to come too."

"Okay," Rowena agreed

***

Amber and Nayan, Shimla 1949

"Who is this Miss Amber that Rowena keeps talking about?" Nayan asked his mother. "Why is Rowena suddenly so attached to her? I have never heard her talking about this person before. Rowena is a young girl. Why is an old lady trying to be a little girl's friend?"

"Amber Mehra is the vice principal of Rowena's new school. She is not old and Rowena likes her."

"But why is the vice principal taking such an interest in a little girl?"

Nayan was thinking of the many people who had tried to take advantage of him by asking his mother or his family for favors from him.

"Amber Mehra is not what you are thinking." Mrs. Kapoor denied, reading her son's expression clearly. Her family is quite well to do. Amber's husband was the president of a bank in Lahore. Amber and her children came to Shimla just before the partition was announced. Her husband followed, but he never made it back. He is believed to be missing or dead. Amber's mother-in-law told me that after they heard the news, it was Amber who kept the family together. She seems like a calm and levelheaded person. I think the vice principal thought that Rowena needed help, and reached out to her."

"Umm, this woman appears to be doing more than is required of her position," Nayan mused.

"Amber Mehra loves the students. She is an educator. You should be pleased. She has turned our little Rowena's life around. Rowena was fighting with her school friends every day.

"In her own gentle way, Miss Amber has put an end to that. You should meet her. She feels that Rowena needs greater parental attention. She might be able to give you a few tips on how to deal with your daughter," his mother replied shaking her head.

"Rowena doesn't need *dealing*. She is a beautiful child. Don't you think I am a good father?" asked Nayan aggrievedly.

"You are, but you need to spend more time with Rowena. She needs you."

"I know, Ma, but I have the business to take care of. What can I do?" Nayan asked, frustrated.

"But Rowena needs you, too," she said gently.

Nayan went to bed that night thinking of his daughter and Amber Mehra. Who was this woman? How had she ingratiated herself into his family's lives? He knew about independent women like her. On the surface they appeared strong and able to take care of themselves. But at the same time, they were looking for rich husbands who would take care of their needs. His mother was a little naïve, he thought. He could deal with a woman like Amber Mehra. He would see her the very next day.

At 10 a.m. he was at his daughter's school asking to see the vice principal. He was guided to her office, but she wasn't there.

"Mrs. Mehra is visiting classrooms this morning," he was told.

"When will she be free?" he asked.

"Probably at recess. Do you have an appointment?" the clerk in Amber's office asked.

"No. Would you tell her I am waiting in her office?" Nayan asked impatiently. He did not like to wait. Ten minutes later, Amber walked in, and Nayan stopped breathing.

She folded her hands in front of her. "*Namaste*, how may I help you?"

"I'm Nayan Kapoor, Rowena's father," Nayan said standing up to return her greeting.

A dimpling smile of friendliness curved Amber's mouth. "Your daughter is charming. How may I help you?"

For the first time in his life, Nayan was dumbstruck. In one moment, Amber's dark, auburn hair, her beautiful and warm, amber eyes, and that dimple, had erased all of Nayan's preconceived prejudices. With one glance, one brief, all encompassing look, Amber's features become engraved on his heart. He wanted to protect and cherish her.

Amber had a glow about her. Nayan didn't know how to act, or what to say. After his wife's death, he had thrown himself into his work. He'd loved the cut and thrust of business and the satisfaction of achieving his goals. Women had not played an important part in his life. Since his wife had died, he had never felt this protective male emotion towards anyone as he was feeling for the woman sitting in front of him. He frowned and took on a distancing business-like tone.

"I heard that my daughter has been getting into trouble with her teacher and some students. Would you tell me what happened?"

Amber looked at him curiously and told him gently, "I think Rowena is fine now. She had some problems adjusting to the new school. A change like that is difficult for anyone. But Rowena is young and resilient. She will be okay."

"I sent Rowena to my mother's because I bought some hotels recently and have to travel to those locations to check on the running and refurbishing of the establishments. I thought she would do well with the stability that my mother's presence would provide.

Nayan leaned forward towards Amber, "When we lived in New Delhi, I was with her every day. I took her to school every morning and brought her back in the afternoon. She stayed alone with the nanny for a few hours but I was home in the evenings. She was well behaved and happy, I believe," Nayan frowned.

"Rowena is very bright and can be a charming little girl," Amber replied. "But she needed to make a place for herself in this school. Many of the students have developed close relationships over the years. I am sure Rowena will too. She is close to one little girl and I am sure she will develop more friendships. It just takes a little time."

Nayan nodded. "I think you are right. I also need to spend more time with her than I have been able to give her. She needs love, but she also needs discipline. My mother, bless her for being there for us, adores her and happily gives in to all her demands."

Amber laughed. "She does. I have met her. She is very kind and loving *and* Rowena can spin her around her little finger. Isn't it Rowena's birthday in two weeks? You could have a party for her and invite her classmates. That will help to break the ice."

"That's right. Her birthday is coming up. I was thinking of taking her to the skating rink, but I think a party is a better idea," Nayan replied, relaxing a little.

"Wait. Here is a list of her classmates," Amber said. "Rowena can write the invitations herself. I also have the phone number and address of a young man who came to our school last month. He entertained the students with card tricks. If you like, you can contact him to entertain the girls at Rowena's party."

"That's a great idea!" exclaimed Nayan laughing.

Amber smiled back.

Nayan looked at Amber's face. The woman was beautiful. Even with the absence of make-up, her face was flawlessly lovely. Her eyes were clear and very kind, but he noted sadness there as well. "Well thank you so much for your time. You have been very helpful. I would like to learn, from an educator's point of view, a little more about the development of a ten-year- old girl. May I take you out for dinner tomorrow evening? We can discuss some strategies."

"I don't think that will be necessary. Every child is different. If you have any questions, you may call me at school." Amber's voice had cooled.

Nayan could tell that he had stepped over an invisible line that no one was allowed to cross. What had he done? Why had he done it? He was an idiot. In his eagerness to get to know this woman, he had rushed in like a fool. He wanted to explain himself, to excuse himself, but a teacher who needed to speak to Amber, interrupted them.

Nayan decided to stroll around the campus to check out this school that his daughter had joined this year. The walls were blessed with paintings of saints. There were sculptures of a baby Jesus with his mother, Mary. At the end of a hallway, there was a sculpture of Christ, crucified on a wooden cross. Paintings of St. Francis of Assisi talking to his followers, and of Saint Anthony granting miracles were hung on the walls. It was strange that in spite of all the fighting for domination between Pakistan and India, here in this small school, in a hill town, flanked by the majestic Himalayan mountain range, young girls of all religions coexisted.

The students were at recess and Nayan searched the playground to find his daughter, but he could not see her anywhere. Then he spotted her sitting under a tree with cute, plump, rosy-cheeked girl with curly brown hair. They were giggling as they played a string game. He had seen Rowena playing *Cat's Cradle* before. Nayan relaxed to see his daughter playing and not getting into any fights. He walked up to the two girls and crouched down next to them, smiling.

"Papa!" Rowena squealed in delight. "This is my friend, Sonia. Remember, I told you about her?"

Nayan nodded. He gave both girls a hug. "I am so glad you two are friends. You must come over to our house soon, Sonia. You may bring your parents or anyone else you want. We would love to have you."

Sonia nodded solemnly, "Okay. I'll ask Mummy."

***

The next day, Rowena returned home from school with her nanny and her friend, Sonia. "*Dadi!* I brought my friend, Sonia, with me. Her mommy says it is okay for her to visit. Her mommy will come to take her home at six o'clock."

Rowena's grandmother welcomed Sonia with a loving smile. "I have milk and toast ready for both of you."

"Okay, *Dadi*," Rowena replied. "Then I am going to teach Sonia how to play *Scrabble*."

Both the girls ran into the house, dropping their satchels near the front door and entered the dining room.

After they had their snack, Rowena took her friend to her room.

"Wow! You have so many toys, Rowena. You even have a bear with glass eyes. I have been asking my mummy to get me one. You are so lucky," Sonia enthused.

"We can share this bear," Rowena said. "Why don't you take it home with you for a week? Then you can return it to me."

"May I? Are you sure? Your grandmother won't object?" Sonia asked uncertainly.

"I'm sure she won't," Rowena replied with a grin.

Sonia hugged the bear to her chest and closed her eyes.

"Come, I'll teach you how to play *Scrabble*. My father brought me a new game. You can bring the bear with you."

Rowena pulled out the game, and after teaching Sonia the rules, they spent two wonderful hours playing the game.

Nayan stopped by to see how the two girls were doing. "You two having fun?" he asked.

"Yes," they both chorused.

Nayan was about to leave them to enjoy the game when he remembered the party. "Rowena, would you like to have a birthday party? he asked. "Miss Amber thought you might."

"That would be so much fun!" Sonia squealed.

"Miss Amber wants me to have a party? She wants to come?" Rowena asked.

"We'll invite her. Then it is up to her."

"But, did she say she wanted to come?" Rowena asked anxiously.

"No. She just thought you might enjoy a party. She gave me a list of all your classmates. We can invite them all."

"Okay, that will be nice," Rowena answered.

Rowena's reply was not enthusiastic, but Nayan went to find his mother to discuss the birthday party. Now that the idea had been placed in his mind, he wanted to set his plans in motion. He had to fly to Calcutta for a few days, but he would be back in Shimla for the party. He found her in the living room, knitting a sweater for Rowena.

"*Ammi*, Rowena's birthday is coming up."

His mother looked up, smiling. "Why do you think I am working so hard on this sweater? I want it ready for her birthday."

"What do you think about a birthday party for Rowena?"

"Oh. But who should we invite?" his mother asked. "She doesn't have many friends. You were thinking of taking her skating. You can take Rowena and Sonia. Rowena would like that."

"Miss Amber suggested inviting her classmates as a way of helping Rowena get to know them in a different environment. We would get to meet the parents as well," Nayan said.

"Oh yes, you went to talk to Miss Amber the other day. You never told me what you talked about."

"We talked about Rowena, of course. She said that it takes time to cultivate friendships, but one way to bring her closer to her classmates would be to invite them to our house," Nayan replied.

"Actually, it sounds like a great idea, now that I look at it from Miss Amber's point of view. We can call the balloon-*walla*. He can blow balloons into different shapes," his mother enthused.

"Miss Amber also suggested we call this man who does card tricks."

"That's great!" his mother exclaimed, "We can get both. I'm sure the party will be a hit. Actually, I invited Amber's family over for tea tomorrow. Mrs. Mehra has accepted. I hope Miss Amber and her daughter come too."

***

The Mehra family was sitting at the dinner table, when Amber's mother-in-law announced that she had

77

accepted an invitation to tea at Rowena's grandmother's house. "Mrs. Kapoor said her son, Rowena's father, was in town. Amber, maybe you can help him with ideas about how he can help his daughter?"

"He visited my office a few days ago and we talked about Rowena for a while. I told him to call me at the office if he had any problems. And I'm sorry *Ammi*," Amber said shaking her head, "I won't be able to come with you. I have to complete all the teachers' *observation reviews*. The end of the school year is around the corner. I need to have them completed and ready for the typist, by Monday."

"I understand. The year-end is always a busy time. Nina, you'll come won't you?" her grandmother asked.

"Sure, I'll come," Nina replied. Her grandfather agreed to go also.

***

Nayan couldn't hide his disappointment when he saw three people walking towards his house, and Amber was not one of them. They must be Amber's in-laws and Amber's daughter. As they came closer, he realized that the daughter would be an image of her mother when she grew older. The resemblance was uncanny.

Rowena screamed when she saw Nina coming. She ran to hug her.

Nina laughed and tried to pick her up but couldn't. "You're heavy," Nina laughed again.

After the greetings were over, Nayan's mother guided them into her house. The sweet smell of Darjeeling Orange Pekoe wafted through the living room.

"Your tea smells delicious," Mrs. Mehra exclaimed.

"Thank you. We came to your home uninvited but you made us feel so welcomed. I wanted to return some of your hospitality. Also, I'd like you to meet my son, Nayan. He came from New Delhi a few days ago."

Nayan bowed low to touch the older couple's feet, and touched his hand to his heart, a sign of respect for elders. He said, "*Namaste*, welcome to our home."

Mr. and Mrs. Mehra offered Nayan their blessings, "*Jeete raho, beta*, Live long son."

"Nina, I will teach you how to play a new game," Rowena interrupted.

"Not today," her grandmother chided. "Today, we will all sit together, talk and enjoy tea."

"May I have tea, also?" Rowena asked happily.

Her grandmother always kept her away from this *grownups* brew, giving her milk or *Horlicks* instead.

"Sure, today you may try the tea," her grandmother smiled.

Nayan turned to Nina. "Your mother could not come?"

"No," Nina smiled regretfully. "This is a busy time of the year for her. She observes the teachers in the classroom all year. But at the end of the year she has to turn in teacher evaluations for each one. She tells them what they are doing well and how they can improve." Nina laughed, "It seems that it isn't just the students who take final exams. The teachers do, too!"

"Nina," I'm going to have a birthday party!" Rowena exclaimed. "You must come."

Nina smiled. "Who are you inviting?"

"We are inviting all her classmates and, of course, you and your family," Nayan interjected.

"Oh no! I have seen some of Rowena's classmates! They are a pretty crazy bunch," Nina exclaimed.

"But you'll come?" Rowena asked anxiously.

Nayan smiled, "Please come. It will mean so much to Rowena, and you can help me with suggestions for games the girls can play."

"Okay," Nina conceded, "Just for you, Rowena. I will make a list of games you can play with your friends and give the list to you in school."

"Why don't Rowena and I walk over to your house say, on Friday, and you can give me the list and also explain how they are played," Nayan suggested.

"That's a great idea," said Nina's grandmother who had heard the conversation. All of you must have tea with us as well."

Nina and her grandparents had walked over for tea as they lived only a short distance away. After they took their leave from the Kapoor's, they began their walk home. They had just reached the main road when they noticed the darkened rain clouds in the bruised sky.

"Let's get a cycle rickshaw," exclaimed Mrs. Mehra. "I think it is about to rain." A cycle rickshaw was a three-wheeled, three-passenger car, propelled by a bicycle. This was a common means of transport in the hill cities. There was not a single rickshaw in sight.

Mr. Mehra looked around. The sweet smell of roasted corncobs from a street vendor filled his senses. "Look some vendors are leaving already. They are hill people; they know when it is going to rain. Maybe we'll find a *dandi*."

"Oh no!" exclaimed Nina, "I don't want to be carried on the shoulders of four men!"

A *dandi* was another common form of transportation in Shimla. A *dandi* did not run on wheels. Its body resembled an easy chair, at the corners of which were horizontal poles supporting the roof. It was covered with canvas cloth to keep out the rain. Two porters, in the front and rear, placed the poles on their shoulders to carry the passengers in the chair.

"That's how they make a living," admonished her grandmother. "If we don't use their transport, they don't make any money. But why are we arguing? I don't see a *dandi* in sight. Maybe if we hurry, we'll miss the downpour. I think all the people are trying to find shelter. We won't find any transport now."

The darkened clouds became alive and volatile. Flocks of birds took to the air in panic. The lightening sparkled in the sky. The three had not gone too far, when the clouds burst and fat drops began to fall. It wasn't just scattered drops. Nina thought she might drown under the avalanche of water. Just then Nina saw a white car approaching them. The driver was Nayan. He had driven after them when it started to rain.

"Get in. I'll drop you home. I didn't want you to get wet," Nayan said smiling.

"Your car will get ruined. We are drenched!" Mrs. Mehra exclaimed.

"Don't worry, just get in."

The three scrambled in with grateful thanks.

Nayan dropped them under their front porch but did not come into the house when invited. "I should get home before this weather worsens." He shook his head regretfully.

Sameer

When the wet trio entered the house, they found Amber sitting in the living room with a young man about Murad's age. He stood up smiling when he saw the three walking in.

"*Ammi,* Papa, Sameer arrived fifteen minutes ago. He is here on a Thomas Cook travel convention. His family moved from Karachi to Bombay," Amber said with a broad smile.

Sameer bent down to touch the older couple's feet, but they pulled him up. Each of them gave him a tight hug.

Mrs. Mehra held Sameer in front of her. Her eyes were wet. "Let me look at you. It's so good to see you. You are just like my Murad."

"Amber told me about Murad," Sameer said sadly. "I am so sorry. Murad *bhai* and I were like brothers, always close, even though we did not see each other that often."

"Yes, when Murad could not be found by the authorities, they presumed he was deceased," Mr. Mehra replied shaking his head sadly.

"We wondered about all of you," Amber's mother-in-law wept. "You were in Karachi and during the time of the partition we couldn't reach your family by phone. The phone lines were never clear."

"It is natural to worry about your only brother, Aunty, but Papa and *Ammi* are quite safe. And so are my wife and my daughters," Sameer said softly.

Amber ushered them all in to sit down.

Nina

Nina looked at her uncle, wide-eyed. He looked so much like her father. She missed the warmth and love of her beloved Papa so much and felt a knot forming in her heart. Nina had tried to stay strong for her mother and her brother, Neil. But at this moment her heartache overwhelmed her. She needed to be by herself for a few moments. "Excuse me, I'm wet from the rain. I'll go change. I'll be right back. Should I bring towels for you to dry yourselves?" she asked her grandparents. They nodded.

Back in her room, Nina fell on her bed and let her tears flow. It had been so long since she had cried. She needed to do this for herself. After a few moments, she went to the bathroom to wash her face and dry herself. She changed and returned with towels for her grandparents.

Amber looked at her daughter with some concern but didn't say anything. She would talk to her when they were alone. Nina handed the towels to her grandparents.

Sameer's Family

Sameer continued with his story. "Papa did not want to leave Karachi. There were no riots or killings in our city. Ayub Khuhro, Sindh's premier, and other Sindhi leaders wanted to retain Sindh's minorities. If the Sindhi Hindus left, Karachi would lose all its merchants and bankers! In Karachi, there were nearly an equal number of Hindus and Muslims with smaller minority groups of Christians, Parsis, and Sikhs. We all worked well together."

Sameer went on. "*Ammi* and Papa felt that we, Sindhi Hindus, were safe. Moreover our family is so fair skinned, we were often mistaken for the British. But then all the refugees from Eastern Punjab started to move into refugee camps in Karachi. Many of the them were angry about having to leave their homes, so they stormed into Hindu homes and threw the Hindus out."

Amber nodded. "The fighting in Sindh was not for religious domination but a need for space."

"Absolutely. That was when Papa decided it was time for us to move to India."

"How did you come to Bombay?" Mrs. Mehra asked. "By ship?"

Sameer laughed. "Aunty, you won't call what we came in, a ship. It was a goods freighter. But even for that, there was a wait list. In the end, we just bribed our way. We left everything behind, except a few precious belongings, and moved. We were told there would be no room. The transport was there for saving lives. So even if we took all our belongings, they would be confiscated at the docks."

Nina had never sailed. "What was it like to sail?" Nina asked. "Did you feel safe?"

Sameer smiled at his young niece. She had inherited Amber's gentle beauty, he noted. "The freighter was overcrowded. We sat on the deck with our belongings. It was safe to sail because there were no stops where the rioters could kill. But the waters were turbulent. My wife, and one of my daughters were sick during the whole journey. It was not comfortable." Sameer smiled, "I would love for you to meet my daughters. You must come to Bombay soon."

Nina smiled back, feeling some of her ache leaving her. "I would like that."

"Did you find work right away?" Amber asked.

"You remember Papa and I worked at the American travel company, Thomas Cook? He was the chairman at the company and I was a regional manager. We carried with us, great references, so we were sure we would find work with that agency in Bombay.

"But unfortunately it wasn't as easy as it seemed. The moment we reached Bombay, after having all our belongings checked minutely, the dock authorities asked where we wanted to go. They asked us if we had any relatives that we could go to in Bombay. If not, they would provide us with a train ticket to a refugee camp out of city. Bombay was too crowded and the officials had been ordered to guide us out of the city."

"So where did you and your family go? You should have come here," Mrs. Mehra said.

"I know, we could have come to you. But we weren't sure there was a Thomas Cook in a small town like Shimla. We were familiar with Bombay, because Papa and I traveled to this city frequently. We didn't want to be sent to some unknown place," Sameer replied.

"What did you do?" Nina's interest was awakened. This seemed like such an adventure. She had thought her train ride had been frightening and exciting, but her uncle's story seemed even more harrowing.

"Papa and I left our luggage at the train station where we had been taken and went to look for jobs. The women stayed with the luggage. We slept at the station for twelve days until the authorities ordered us out.

Then we remembered Uncle Vinay in Poona. So we asked to get train tickets to Poona. Uncle welcomed us, but his accommodations were meager. Our family of six all lived in one small room. Fortunately, in one month we received an answer from the Thomas Cook agency at the Taj Mahal Hotel. Both of us were invited to work there. The hotel would provide us with accommodations. We took the jobs. We left Poona to return to Bombay."

"I am so happy for all of you," Mrs. Mehra said teary eyed. "Are there any problems in Bombay with rioters?"

"In pockets of Bombay, there are uprisings now and again. But the police and the Indian government have tried to control the unrest," Sameer replied. "Shimla is relatively untouched by the politics, Aunty, even though it used to be the summer capital for the British."

"Yes, we hear of problems continuing in the big cities. But here we see it only occasionally," his aunt replied. "You must be hungry. Let me talk to the cook about having dinner served."

Mrs. Mehra went to the kitchen to ask the cook to lay out the meal.

Dinner with Sameer was a time of reconnecting family ties. He told them that his two daughters, fifteen and fourteen, were attending a local school and his wife, who was a pharmacist in Karachi, had found a job at *Unichem*, a pharmaceutical company. They had bought a house near the hotel. His mother took care of 'home affairs,' as Sameer called it. Their life, once again gave them a sense of normality.

When Sameer left that night, the rain had stopped. Mrs. Mehra gave him a box of sesame seed *laddus* (a ball shaped sweet filled with walnuts). "Your father loved these when he was young. I made them yesterday." She also gave him a box of chocolates for his daughters. "Give your family my love and tell them they are always in our thoughts."

Sameer hugged each member goodbye, but he held Nina in his arms for longer. He felt so sorry for this young girl who must miss her father very much. "Come to visit soon," he told her.

That night when Amber and her daughter were alone, Amber gave Nina a hug. "You know I love you, my sweet one? You have gone through so much during the last two years and yet you have taken the changes bravely."

"I know you love me, *Ammi*. But sometimes I miss Papa so much. It hurts," Nina whispered.

Amber smiled sadly. "When you saw your uncle, Sameer... he looks so much like your father, thoughts of Papa must have flooded you with emotion. I felt it too. I saw your face when you left the room and when you came back. I knew you must have been crying." Amber hugged her again. "I wish I could bring your papa back to us. But now we have to put our faith in God. Only God knows why life makes us face challenges. Would you like to pray with me?"

"Yes, *Ammi*," Nina replied in a soft voice. "I would like that very much." Amber guided her to the small altar in their room. She lit a candle in front of the statue of Lord Krishna and the goddess Lakshmi. They both prayed. They could hear the rain on the roof. It had started again. It seemed, with that rain, had come an answering blessing.

***

Rowena's birthday party was a success. The birthday parties of Rowena's classmates had been simple affairs. Most of them had cake, sandwiches, pastries, a few games like *Pin the Tail on the Donkey*, or relay races. The addition of the card trick performer had her school friends in awe. The man who twisted a balloon into different shapes for each guest delighted them. The presence of their vice principal at their classmate, Rowena's house, surprised them. Maybe Rowena wasn't a person to be shunned after all.

"Your party is so much fun!" Rowena's friend Sonia exclaimed.

"Rowena, would you like to come Christmas caroling with us next month?" asked a classmate. "My parents go for Christmas mass on December twenty fourth. After that we go caroling down Mall Road and even visit some of the parishioners' homes where they serve us hot chocolate."

"I'll ask," replied Rowena. "What is a parishioner?"

"Oh just people that go to our Catholic church. We have learned so many carols. It is fun to go out to sing," her friend replied.

"Will you come to my birthday party?" asked another. "My birthday is in two weeks."

"Will you toboggan with us, when the first snow falls?" asked still another. "My parents, my brother and I always go sliding down hills."

88

Rowena was delighted and a little confused by all the invitations. In her mind, she connected them, somehow, to Nina, who helped with all the games, and Miss Amber. She turned to Nina to give her a hug.

"I love you, Nina. You are my best friend."

Nina looked down at the young girl, surprised, but she smiled. "Are you having fun, Rowena?"

"Yes, and it's all because of you. You are so good with all the games. I always have fun, when you are there. We are alike, you know? You are an only daughter, and I am too," Rowena grinned.

Nina ruffled the younger girl's hair. "Yes, but I do have a brother."

"You do? Where is he?" Rowena asked.

"Neil is studying in England. He will graduate next year," Nina replied.

"Oh, I have always wanted to go to England. I want to go there to meet Jesus."

"Jesus?"

"Jesus Christ. He came from the Holy Land like all the nuns at our school. Our nuns are from England, the Holy Land," Rowena replied.

"No, my cutie." Nina turned to Rowena with a smile. "England is not the Holy Land. The Holy Land is where Christ was born and where he grew up. Christ was not born in England. He was born in Bethlehem. He grew up in Nazareth. Our nuns believe in his teachings. They are Catholics."

Nayan, who had heard part of the conversation, interrupted them. "Rowena is confused. I will talk to her."

"Don't worry, these confusions are common. When I was Rowena's age, I wanted to be a nun because I thought all nuns were saints. When they are ordained, they take on the names of saints; Mother Saint Agnes, Mother Saint Beatrice, Mother Saint Camilla, Mother Saint Lourdes. I thought becoming a nun was a fast way to sainthood," Nina explained with a smile.

Nayan grinned at her. "Okay. I'll stay out of this."

"Nina, is your brother in school or college?" Rowena asked.

"He's in college, studying economics and finance."

"Your mother seems to know all the students' parents so well!" Nayan had turned his attention to Amber who was talking animatedly to two of the parents.

"She does," Nina replied. Her office is an open house. Parents feel free to talk to her whenever they need. She invites them to the school three times a year for a dinner. All the teachers and the Mother Superior are there. The parents can talk and ask questions about the school program. They can discuss any student's problem. The parents and the school staff get to know each other quite well during these meetings.

"She has changed the way our school is run. Before my mother joined the school, report cards were mailed out after the school closed. Parents would then find out if their child had passed or failed. Sometimes it was a shock. She changed all that," Nina said proudly.

"Oh, how did she do that?" asked Nayan interestedly.

"The teachers see each parent before school closes. The parents check their child's report card. At this time they can ask any questions they may have. Then they sign the progress reports. The parents like that."

"I bet right now they are asking her how their children are doing!" Nayan exclaimed.

"And my mother can tell them exactly how they are doing because she checks the report cards and test scores of every student."

Nayan looked at Amber. Amber was as polished and refined as the gem whose name she bore. A fire lurked within her. She talked to each parent with warmth and charm. She was beautiful. Her high, classic cheekbones, small straight nose, and perfectly formed lips were designed to turn heads wherever she went. She didn't have the glamorous looks of a fashion model or a movie star, but she had everything he desired.

He was about to join her and the two parents, when he met the Seths and his friend Rajat Roy. Mrs. Seth was wagging a finger at Rajat as if she was trying to poke holes in Rajat's argument. Rajat signaled to Nayan, needing a fourth party to intervene.

"All I said was that the police could not convict the brothers because they did not kill their sister. She killed herself," Rajat said excusing his earlier comments.

Mrs. Seth repeated the story of a young Hindu Bengali woman who had married a Muslim man. They had one daughter. At the time of the partition they had decided to leave for East Pakistan. But before they could cross the border, the woman's brothers kidnapped their sister and brought her back with them. They left her daughter with the father.

The man was unable to console or take care of

his daughter. He begged a Hindu couple returning to the Indian side to take his daughter to her mother. The couple claimed the girl was their daughter to the border authorities and left her with her mother when they reached Calcutta.

The brothers refused to accept a child of half Muslim blood. They mistreated both of them so much that one day the woman picked up her daughter and jumped into a nearby well, drowning them both. The police had not taken any action against the brothers.

Mrs. Seth said the government should pass laws against such mistreatment of women. It was the women who suffered.

Nayan nodded his head in agreement. "Absolutely. The partition has resulted in millions of lost lives, but women have taken the brunt of its violence. The government has done a lot to help the people in Punjab, but on the Bengal side it is still chaotic. I just returned from Calcutta last night. The city is getting congested. Migrants are still coming from East Pakistan. There is not enough being done to resettle and rehabilitate the refugees."

"My parents live there. They also tell me the city is overflowing with migrants," Rajat confirmed.

"The partition between West Pakistan and India was bad, but the partition in the East was absolutely thoughtless. The people of the area look alike and speak the same language. Eastern and Western Bengal worked well together. They just practiced different religions." Nayan couldn't keep the frustration from his voice.

"Yes," said Mr. Seth. "At least in Punjab the Pakistanis profited from the rich land left on their side, but in Bengal, both India and Pakistan lost. All the jute grows in East Pakistan, but the factories making sacks and cloth out of the raw material are in India. All the rice grown in Bengal is in India. The eastern side is starving. The industry and commerce is in West Bengal. East Pakistan has been cut off."

"There have been so many riots, I have asked my parents to move in with us," said Rajat. "They are old now. I am afraid their home may be seized by vandals. They won't be able to protect themselves from the violence," said Rajat.

"I agree, it would be best to bring your parents to live with you," said Nayan and then excused himself to join Amber and the other parents in her group. A parent was praising Amber for instituting monthly walks where the girls learned about the indigenous plants, birds, and the wildlife of Shimla from experts.

"Even I didn't know the names of the trees on our hillsides. My daughter taught me about *sisham*, Indian rosewood, *chir* pine and deodar or cedar trees. She taught me how the beautiful rhododendron is such an amazing plant and so important to the ecology of the area. She told me that by attracting insects which in turn attract birds, rhododendrons form a major link in the high altitude ecosystems," a parent told her proudly.

Amber smiled. "I want the students to be aware of their surroundings and how they can protect the nature around them."

"Oh, and my daughter especially enjoys *Environment Week*."

This was something new that Amber had started. The students left their classrooms to learn for the outdoors. This was a time for them to go trekking into the mighty Himalayan ranges. They could learn outdoor photography. They could also stay close to home and explore the hillsides of Shimla under the watchful eye of a well-qualified instructor.

Amber nodded smiling. "I want our students to learn resourcefulness. I want them to learn how to work together. This bonding often leads to life-long friendships."

Nayan listened to this conversation in surprise. He had not realized Amber had made so many changes at the school. There was a strength and force behind this beautiful, gentle woman with whom he realized he was falling in love.

***

All through the afternoon, Amber was increasingly aware of being observed by Nayan Kapoor. He stood with them not saying a great deal, but he listened to every word she said. Why was he watching her every move? Why was he listening to her as if what she said mattered to him? He was making her feel self conscious.

Amber reminded the parents about the end of the year recital. They all agreed they were looking forward to it.

The party drew to an end, and the young guests said reluctant goodbyes. Rowena hugged each guest happily. Mr. and Mrs. Mehra, Amber and Nina, also said their goodbyes. Rowena hugged Nina and thanked her for all her help.

***

The next morning, Rowena left for school after breakfast, but Nayan and his mother lingered over their tea. His mother looked at him, smiling. "I think everything went well, don't you think?" Nayan didn't reply, deep in his own thoughts.

"What is it, Nayan?" His mother watched him with smiling puzzlement.

He looked up from his teacup, frowning. "Sorry, *Ammi,* I didn't hear your question."

Her mouth quirked. "You take your tea black, with no sugar, and yet for some reason you've been stirring the bottom out of your cup for the last five minutes!" she said pointedly.

He looked down at the submerged spoon, dropping it into the saucer realizing she was right. He shook his head. "I was just thinking."

"What about?"

"*Ammi,* you've often encouraged me to get married again, but I was too busy with work to even think of that. But now, as you said, the business is falling into place. Rowena needs a mother. I think I should get married."

"That's an excellent idea," his mother told him approvingly. "I'll start looking for a suitable wife for you, and a mother for Rowena."

"No, no!" Nayan rejected the idea emphatically. "I don't want that sort of marriage. I'll marry someone I want to be with for the rest of my life."

"Would that somebody be Amber?" asked his mother with an amused smile.

"You guessed? But how?"

"I'm your mother. I've seen how you look at her, with admiration and respect. I've seen how you talk to her daughter, Nina. It's almost as if you consider her your own daughter. I saw the way you panicked when it started to rain on the day the Mehras were over for tea. You didn't wait for the driver. You rushed out yourself.

You were concerned for her family."

"We haven't known each other very long. I know I like her but I don't know how she feels about me. I think she likes me but I don't quite know how to ask her."

"Maybe I can help."

Ammi please don't do anything. Let me think. I'll find a way."

***

November, the end of the school year, meant the nights turned clear and brilliant and the temperatures grew cold enough to make one realize that winter was fast approaching. The cicadas fell silent, shed their skins, while their exoskeletons clung to the twigs of trees, emptied of life. The rain was gentler. There was none of the fury, but a quieter patter sounded on the corrugated tin roofs.

Nayan and Rowena came over to the Mehra house the day after the party to thank them for coming to the party, for their help, and for the gifts for Rowena. Amber had picked a game of *Carrom* for her. She also gave her a lovely dress made by a seamstress who designed girls' dresses. It was a beautiful red and white hand-smocked dress. Amber knew Rowena would look good in it.

When Nayan got Amber to himself for a few moments, he thanked her again.

"I want to thank you, for all you have done for Rowena. The idea of the party was brilliant. Rowena has changed so much just by being close to you and Nina. I also want to commend you for all the changes you have brought about at the school in such a short time."

"Thank you," Amber smiled. "I've always known the kind of school, I would have wanted for myself. School is not just about book learning. I would have loved to have learned life skills, an appreciation of my environment, and respect for human beings in my school."

"I can see you are an admirable and unusual woman. I feel lucky to know you," Nayan said.

Amber felt her face flushing. She turned to him in surprise. "Thank you."

Nayan ignored the look in her eyes and the incredulity in her voice. "Rowena and I are both fortunate to know you. I have never met a person like you. I hope we can be friends," Nayan said.

"Friends?"

"*Good* friends," Nayan said smiling. Amber's face flushed and her eyes widened as she recognized the male appreciation in his eyes.

"I guess so," Amber said hesitatingly, not sure where this could go. After her marriage to Murad, Amber had never thought of another man in the same way.

"May we shake hands on that?" Nayan asked. Amber gave him her hand.

***

A moment later, Mr. Mehra entered the house returning from his walk. "Hello. Good to see you Nayan, *beta*. The birthday party was great. I enjoyed myself."

"Thank you, Mr. Mehra. We are all glad you came, and Nina was such a big help with the games."

"Call me 'Uncle.' We know each now. You are right, Nina was very good. Talking about games, do you play chess by any chance? My friend and I played

97

everyday, but now he has left Shimla to live with his son and his family. I would love to have a partner."

"I'm not here all the time. But sure, Uncle, when I'm in Shimla, I'll play with you," Nayan replied smiling.

"How about now? Do you have time now?" Mr. Mehra asked eagerly.

"Er... okay I guess I can play one game," replied Nayan as Mr. Mehra led him to the chessboard table.

Rowena was with Nina in her room. Despite the age difference the two girls got on well together, almost like sisters. Amber decided she could finish some of the schoolwork she had brought home.

Across the room she could see Nayan playing chess, frowning in concentration as he thought of his next move. He was very good looking, she thought. He was caring too. He wanted the best for his mother and daughter. Nina seemed to like him. At the party, Nayan had spent a lot of time with Nina, Amber had noticed.

Nayan looked up suddenly, as if he sensed that she was watching him. His eyes locked with hers for a moment. Then he looked back at the board.

***

That night Amber lay in bed staring at the ceiling. Her marriage to Murad had been happy and fulfilling. They had loved each other. She knew that if Murad was with her, she would not have responded to Nayan.

She sat up abruptly and turned on the bedside lamp. On the dresser was a photo of Murad with Neil and Nina. Their faces smiled at her. Tears rushed into her eyes, blurring her vision. She brought the photo closer and kissed Murad.

"You were my first love, Murad. I fell in love

with you almost as soon as I met you. But you are not with me, and I'm afraid I've begun to have feelings for another man," Amber wept. She let the tears flow. Murad just smiled at her. There was no censure or reproof in his eyes. Amber cried herself to sleep.

The next day was very busy. The school would close in one week. The students felt lighthearted and carefree. They would get a long winter break. The school would be closed for over three months from December 1 until March 15. A few classes were in the playground but there was no Physical Education. This was a time for 'free play.' She heard the girls chanting:

"Bye bye playground
Do not fret,
We will come and see you yet.
Bye bye monkey bars
Do not fret,
We will come and see you yet."

This was the annual tradition. The girls would bid farewell to every object in the school.

"Bye bye walls
Do not fret,
We will come and see you yet
Bye bye toilet paper
Do not fret,
We will come and see you yet."

Amber smiled. The girls were just having fun.

Mother Superior walked in just then. "Amber, Miss Brown says she has not received her class progress reports. Have you checked them yet?"

"Yes, of course. I sent them back to her last week. The office clerk, Sukhdev took them to her. Why didn't she mention it earlier?" Amber asked, astonished.

"Sukhdev," Amber called out to the clerk, "Did you take the progress reports to Miss Brown?"

"Yes, Miss Amber, I did. She was busy, and a little distracted, but I told her I was placing them on her desk."

"Did you place the folder right in front, where she could see it?"

"She had a lot of papers on her desk. I just put the folder on top of the papers."

Mother Superior shook her head. "Miss Brown is a good teacher but absent-minded and disorganized. I am sure it is lost among her pile of papers. I've spoken to her about her clutter. I will talk to her now."

"Mother Superior, please don't worry. I'll go to her myself and help her find them."

Amber walked to Miss Brown's class. She had not wanted Mother Superior to talk to her, because Mother's impatience would only make things worse.

"Hi, Sylvia."

"I'm sorry, Amber. I just remembered, Sukhdev did bring a folder from you, but I can't seem to find it." Sylvia was nearly in tears.

"I'll help you," Amber said calmly. They placed all the papers on the floor and then started sorting them carefully. Luckily Miss Brown's class was on its break. Amber found the folder in minutes.

"Thank you, Amber! I don't know what I would do without you. I promise I will conference with every parent, even if it means working late," she said sincerely.

Amber walked back to her office with a sigh. She was glad she would get a break from this. She would miss the students, and the staff but she needed some time off.

Around 11:30 that morning, she got a surprise when Nayan knocked at her door.

"May I take you out for lunch?"

Amber looked up at him astonished. He hadn't called to tell her he was coming. "Oh no, Nayan. I can't leave. I have worked through most of my lunches this month."

"All the more reason to take a complete break. I promise I'll bring you back in half an hour. There is a new South Indian *dosa* restaurant that has recently opened. I've heard they make great *dosas*. Come. The faster we leave the sooner we'll be back." The idea of taking a break from this mountain of work suddenly seemed tempting.

"Okay," she smiled. "Let's go." She informed the office clerk that she was leaving for lunch and would be back in about half hour. Her heart felt light.

"You were so sure I would come."

"Not at all," said Nayan seriously. "I was very nervous. I knew if I called you ahead of time, you would refuse. I was so nervous, I cut myself shaving. I sprayed shaving foam under my arms. I tried on several shirts before settling on this one. That's how nervous I was."

Amber looked at him. His blue shirt suited him. She laughed delightedly.

The little *dosa* restaurant was quaint. The crepes made with fermented rice and black lentil batter, stuffed with spicy potatoes, were delicious. So was the coconut chutney. The cook was fast. Within minutes of placing their order, they were eating their crisp *dosas*.

101

They ended the meal with the classic South Indian 'yard coffee' or *kaafi* as the South Indians called it. After spooning coffee powder and sugar in boiling milk, the owner himself, served it, pouring the liquid back and forth between two tumblers in huge arc-like motions. This mixed the ingredients and cooled the hot coffee to sipping temperature. It also aerated the mix without adding water, and Amber and Nayan were served cappuccinos, South Indian style.

"The distance between the pouring and the receiving cup gave it the name of yard coffee," explained Nayan smiling.

Amber smiled back. She felt happier today than in the last two years. She had been lost and lonely after Murad had not returned. Work and study had kept her mind occupied, but it had also prevented her from making friends. There had never been any time.

The little time she had, she had spent consoling Murad's parents and watching out for Nina.

A few men had shown an interest in her – the specialist who had come to train the teachers, the sports director, but when she had not shown any interest, nor encouraged them, they left her alone. She felt nothing and nobody appealed to her. Her mother-in-law had once asked her if she would care to marry again. But she'd brushed her suggestion aside. She pushed any thoughts, in that direction, away from her and had concentrated on her work during the day. At night she had fallen into bed, too exhausted to think or worry.

"Do you miss your wife?" Amber asked tentatively.

"I loved my wife," Nayan told her seriously. "She was a beautiful person, kind, thoughtful and generous. But she wasn't granted good health. I wish I could have done something. She discovered she had stage-four ovarian cancer. It had spread to other areas." Nayan looked at Amber. He saw clear compassion. "She lived for two years after the diagnosis, but she suffered too much. I feel guilty I had no time to mourn, because my father died a day after her death. Creditors deluged me. I needed to do something fast. I have been on a speed ride ever since. You are the first person I have ever have had feelings for since that time."

Amber covered his hands with hers. They looked at each other sadly. Both of them had experienced great voids in their lives.

"Amber, I don't know how you feel about me, but I love you. If you don't want to be in a relationship, I'll understand. But if you need help, I'll be there for you. I know you loved Murad. I respect that. I loved my wife. But I've fallen in love with you. Our future is in your hands."

Amber shook her head. "My decision does not depend on me alone. It depends on Nina, Neil, my in-laws, and my parents. I know Nina likes you but Neil has never met you. I have kept my family together for so long. I can't abandon them now."

"I understand, "Nayan replied. "But what about your happiness and mine? Don't you want a partner to share your joys and sorrows? *I* do. I want that partner to be you. I want you to be my wife. I will take care of Nina and Neil. They will be like my daughter and son. "

Amber looked at him wistfully. "I'm sorry I can't answer your question right now, but I will think about it."

Nayan looked at Amber and smiled ruefully. "I

understand," he said, "I won't rush you." He sighed, "our thirty minutes are nearly up. I'll take you back to school."

***

The end-of-year school recital began with Mother Superior hoisting the Indian flag up the pole. The saffron, white, and green tricolor with the blue chakra in the middle, opened in a shower of rose petals. The audience stood up to sing the National Anthem, *Jana, Gana, Mana,* the popular song written by the Bengali poet, Rabindra Nath Tagore. Ten high school girls who played the tune on their wooden flutes accompanied them. The melody of this song, always gave Amber goose bumps. She was surprised to hear two girls standing behind her, giggling.

"You know, my dad told me that George V thought it was written for him. He even thanked Tagore for writing the song for him," said one.

"I know. The king must have been so disappointed when Rabindra Nath Tagore wrote back to say there was a misunderstanding," giggled the other. "He told the king that the mentor and creator of Bharat, India, mentioned in the song, was not George V but God Himself."

The girls from first standard, talked about the meaning of the colors of the Indian flag. Amber smiled. Each girl had memorized her lines and had to speak clearly into the speaker. They looked so proud but she could tell they were nervous.

"We are proud to be part of independent India. This is our *Tiranga,* tricolored flag. The saffron stripe represents courage and selflessness." She handed the microphone to the next student.

"The white stripe in the middle represents honesty, purity, and peace. It represents light and the path of truth." The third girl stepped forward.

"The circular symbol in the middle is the Ashoka *chakra*, the wheel of motion. We are an independent country. We will move forward and progress."

"The green stripe at the bottom stands for fertility and prosperity."

As the four girls finished their speech, they brandished the Indian flag in front of them. "Jai Hind!" Let our land be victorious. They got a resounding applause.

Rowena's class performed a dance depicting parts of the epic, *Ramayana*. As winter was fast approaching, some classes sang Christmas carols and *Jingle Bells*. Nina had a solo performance on the harmonium. She sang a song in her very melodious voice. Amber was so proud of her daughter. Nina had started learning how to play the harmonium when she joined this school two years ago. She played the instrument so well. After they left Lahore she continued to take voice lessons in Shimla.

The recital ended with a speech by Mother Superior. She thanked the audience for attending and she wished the students a safe winter break. She looked forward to seeing them again in March. The recital was followed by a banquet for the students and their families. Many of the parents and the students came to speak to Amber. Some of Nina's friends, along with their families, came to congratulate her. Anjali's brother, Gautam, smiled at Nina.

"You sing beautifully."

Nina smiled back. "Thank you. I was nervous."

Gautam attended the local boys' school, Bishop Cotton, and he had met Nina recently at the Boys and Girls Tea at the Loreto Convent. "Did you get the notes, I sent through Anjali?" he asked Nina urgently. She nodded.

"Why didn't you write back?" he questioned. "I thought Anjali wasn't giving you the notes. I yelled at her yesterday when she told me you were not interested in me!"

"Gautam, I met you for the first time at the School Tea. This is the second time I am meeting you. Did you want us to be pen-friends?"

He flushed. "I fell in love with you when I saw you that day. I want you to be my girlfriend."

"You're crazy, Gautam, life doesn't work that way."

"Life can work that way. I'm crazy? You're right. I *am* crazy about *you*," he replied fiercely.

Anjali joined them then, and that conversation ended. Amber watched her daughter with the young boy. He was tall with dark hair and shining brown eyes.

Nayan was there with his mother. Along with Rowena, they came to talk to Amber and her family. When Nayan was close enough to Amber he whispered, "I'm not giving up on us. I love you."

***

It was the last day of school. There were teary and fond goodbyes. Some of the students would not be back. Many were going to the plains for the winter break to spend their three-month vacation. Amber and Nina planned on visiting Amber's family in New Delhi for two months. School was officially closed. From the

106

grey and red building of Loreto Convent, Amber walked down the hill. Nina skipped along beside her.

"Bye, bye school, I'm not going to fret
    I hope I don't see you for three months yet.
Yea."

She gave her mother a hug. "No more books, no more studying. I will sleep for as long as I want. I'll read all the Sherlock Holmes and Watson mysteries. I'll go on long hikes. Anjali and Mridula want to come. You can come too, Ma."

"Let's just celebrate," said Amber. "Let's stop off at the coffee house and have cold coffee with coffee ice cream and some chicken patties."

"I love chicken patties," Nina drooled. "I would love that." They headed in that direction. They hadn't gone far, when a white car slowed to a stop near them. It was Nayan and a smiling Rowena.

"May we give you a lift home?" asked Nayan.

"Thanks but no. We were just going to stop off at the coffee house for some coffee and chicken patties. You're welcome to join us, if you like," Nina invited.

"I love chicken patties. Can we, can we Papa? Please."

"Sure," said Nayan, laughing.

The coffee house was not far, but the road to it followed the contours of the hill twisting its way around the ridges and ravines. At seven thousand feet above sea level, the restaurant actually looked more like an English cottage sitting on pink white clouds. Wild flowers surrounded the front garden. Dog violets and hooded cobra lilies pushed though tangles of ruby-bright strawberries. A weeping willow and the enormous wisterias decorated and sheltered this beautiful café. A calf casually chomped on some of the greenery.

"Look," said Nayan laughing. "Now you ladies can have fresh milk with your tea or coffee!"

Several customers sat outside in the beautiful garden but there was a chill in the air. The crackling fire, in the restaurant, welcomed the laughing group. A smiling waiter seated them and took their order. Nayan ordered a pot of Darjeeling Lopchu tea. It was getting cooler so Amber ordered the same. Nina stuck to cold coffee with coffee ice cream and Rowena asked for a hot chocolate. They also ordered a large plate of chicken patties.

"Look Miss Amber. We seem to be floating on clouds!" They all looked out of the large restaurant window to see the clouds floating up and down around this pretty country cottage.

"I think I like living in Shimla now, in spite of all the mosquitoes, scorpions, and fleas. I used to miss my friends and my home in New Delhi, but I have made new friends at this school," said Rowena smiling. "Nina, didn't you feel homesick for your friends when you first came here?"

"I did. I hated to leave Lahore. I was born there. I grew up there," Nina replied. "But we were forced to leave. After the partition of India and Pakistan was announced, it became too dangerous for us to live there. There was a curfew on the streets. We couldn't leave our homes after six p.m. We left Lahore on August 12, just two days before Pakistan announced its independence."

"How did you come?" asked Rowena.

Nina hesitated and Amber looked at her silently as she realized her daughter was thinking of her father. "My father arranged for us to take the train. He couldn't come with us but he sent us with body guards,"

"Was the ride scary?"

"Yes it was. We relaxed only after we got on the train from Kalka to Shimla. That was fun!" Nina grinned. "You must ride on that toy train if you haven't. Looking out of the train, my brother, Neil, said it reminded him of the descriptions of Shimla by Rudyard Kipling. Much of Kipling's *Kim* is set here. The train has no doors. It goes at ten miles and hour but it allows you to appreciate the scenery. People get on and off the moving train to pick up tea and snacks on the way."

Nayan poured tea for Amber and himself. "Yes, it is one of the most unique railroads in the world," he said. "The longest tunnel on this route is the Barog tunnel named after the engineer who started the tunnel. He began digging the tunnel from both ends simultaneously only to realize the two ends were not aligned. The British government fined him for wasting government time and money. Mr. Barog felt so humiliated that he shot himself."

"I didn't know that," Nina, Amber, and Rowena chorused.

"Mr. Harrington was given charge to dig a new tunnel about half a mile away."

The conversation flowed as the four had their drinks and ate delicious chicken patties.

"Miss Amber, can Nina come Christmas caroling with me? Martha, one of the girls in my class has asked me to go with her."

"I'm afraid not," Amber replied. She looked affectionately at the young girl. "We are going to New Delhi to visit Nina's grandparents. We haven't seen them for two years."

"Oh, we are going to New Delhi too, aren't we Papa?" asked Rowena. "You said you would take me to visit my friends?"

"Yes, I'll take you and *dadi* to New Delhi." He turned to Amber. "I have a house in New Delhi so I will bring Rowena. Maybe we can all meet."

"Yes, Miss Amber, I would love to spend time with you and Nina," exclaimed Rowena.

"Your father is a lawyer, isn't he?" Nayan asked.

"He has his own practice. He helps refugees get rehabilitated," Amber replied.

"Oh, maybe my friend, Hari, can help him. He is in charge of allotting land and housing to the displaced refugees."

"Are you talking about Hari and Sheila?" asked Amber astonished.

"Yes, do you know them?"

"They are from Lahore. Murad and I knew them well. They invited us to stay with them when we moved to New Delhi. But we never went to New Delhi," Amber replied sadly.

Nayan drove Amber and Nina home. Rowena chattered non-stop. Amber and Nina replied to her questions good-humoredly.

After Nayan and Rowena left, Nina put her arm around her mother, grinning.

"I think Uncle Nayan has a 'thing' for you."

110

"You mean like Anjali's brother, Gautam, has a 'thing' for you?" Amber said slyly, leaving an open-mouthed Nina behind as she walked into the house.

***

New Delhi, December 1949

Amber's parents and her nineteen-year-old sister, Aparna, were at the New Delhi train station to receive them.

"Amber, Nina!" Aparna called when she saw them disembark. She flew across the railway platform and threw herself into Amber's arms. Amber took the impact of her sister's love with a big smile. Then Aparna turned to hug her niece.

"It's been too long. I've missed you." She hugged them both again. By this time Amber's parents had caught up. Her mother sobbed as she hugged her daughter and granddaughter. Tears welled up in her father's eyes as well.

"Come," said Amber's father gruffly his voice filled with emotion. "Let's find you a *coolie*, a porter, to carry your luggage.

In the car, they shared stories of how each family had crossed the border and how their lives had changed so much in the 'new' India.

Amber's mother cried. "We were so shocked to hear about Murad. If only he had crossed the border with you and the children."

"Man proposes, but God disposes," said Amber's father shaking his head quoting the German cleric Thomas Kempis. "We can make all the plans we want, but in the end it's God that directs. Why the partition even took place is also unfathomable. So many lives sacrificed in the mass migrations." They were all quiet for a while.

"How about all of you?" asked Amber turning anxious eyes towards her parents.

There was a pause before her father answered. Mr. Vij pondered how he should answer his daughter's question.

How can I tell my child calmly about the depths into which I fell during that time? That period of my life almost destroyed me. I was supposed to be the strength of my family, but I felt powerless to protect them.

Powerless to stop the forcible move from Pakistan to India; unable to prevent my family from the dangers of that journey; incapable of curbing the starvation my family suffered because of a lack of food and water on their journey.

I failed to control my own fears that we might not survive the journey. The cyanide tablets, or suicide pills, I kept in my pocket, were a protection for my family if they were in danger from abductors. But I really had no control over life or death.

In the refugee camp, reduced to standing in dole lines for clothes, for food, or in hopes of a job, my self-disgust knew no bounds.

Standing in line for food, I remember looking at my wife and daughter standing behind me. The image of those once beautiful human beings, gaunt and emaciated, still haunts me. Their heads were shaved, because of the lice infestation at the camp, and their clothes and shoes were ill fitting. How could I have let this happen to them? I felt emasculated.

I tried to remind myself, it was because of the cards we had been dealt. We were forced to play those cards. How I wish I could live in the present and only

look forward to the future, but the memories of the past haunt me and sometimes overwhelm me.
Should I share those memories? No, of course not. I don't want my darkest moments to become someone else's nightmare. It was bad enough for me to touch bottom. How can I bear to have others know about it?

***

To his daughter, Mr. Vij replied calmly, but with a slight tremor in his voice. "It's over now, my child. We are alive." *Yes, they were. They had all played their cards gracefully.* "I prefer to look at the future, not the past. We have survived. Sarla and her family have found housing in Ludhiana. Your mother and Aparna are safe. You and Nina are with us. I only wish, Murad..."

Amber nodded sadly. "Papa, you don't know how often I wished I had sent the children to Shimla with the guards and accompanied Murad two days later. I might have been able to save him."

Aparna hugged her sister. "No one can change what has happened. I am grateful that you and Nina are finally together with us."

"What is it like now in New Delhi, *Nanu?*" Nina asked her grandfather. "You are helping the refugees get their rights. How is it working out?"

"It could have been worse. There are six refugee camps with 300,000 refugees in the largest camp, the Kingsway Camp. There was vacant land around the city so the government went about building housing for the refugees right away," her grandfather replied. "But they have so many needs. The basic essentials are required to start a new life. They need food, clothes,

113

accommodation, bank accounts, loans, and employment. Some require proof of identity or qualifications. The country has set up a Ministry of Rehabilitation in every state."

"Is the ministry doing a lot for the refugees, *Nanu?*" Nina asked her grandfather.

"They are, my *bitiya*. State sponsored projects have offered loans to businessmen to restart their factories, to resume businesses. Special quotas have been set up to ensure that refugees have priority access to government jobs or a place at the university. But everything takes time. There is so much paperwork and bureaucracy. That is where I come in to help speed up the process," her grandfather replied with a smile. "There is lengthy paperwork which many cannot read. I help them with it."

"Refugees definitely get priority." Aparna agreed with her father. "I got admission at my college, soon after we reached Delhi, just because of the special quotas for refugees. How about both of you? Do you like Shimla?"

"Yes," replied Nina. "We're cocooned in the Himalayan foothills, protected by those majestic peaks, comparatively untouched by all that is happening in Delhi."

"I like my job," said Amber. "It's very interesting, and we are living with Murad's parents. Being with them makes me think Murad will return soon."

Aparna looked at Amber worriedly. She wondered if that was healthy, but didn't say anything.

When they reached the family home, Amber's mother bustled into the house to set the table for dinner, while her father asked the housekeeper to help take the luggage into the house.

Amber and Nina looked at the house with interest. It was nice. It had been freshly painted after the rains. A path from the garden led to a stepped up veranda. Bougainvillea crept up the two roman pillars.

Aparna saw them looking at the house. "I know it is not like our home in Bhakkar. It has only three bedrooms, a drawing room, dining room, and a kitchen. Behind the house, at the end of the backyard, are quarters for the housekeeper.

"Our first house, after we moved out of the refugee camp, in Jalandhar, to Panipat, was a vacated Muslim *haveli*. It was a large brick building with sections of *zenana,* for women, and *mardana* for men, opening to a courtyard. There was a well in the center of the courtyard. We did not have running water or toilets that flush. The rooms were large with high ceilings. In January it used to freeze in that house.

One day we tried to light a fire and the whole room filled up with smoke. When our housekeeper tried to clean the chimney with a long broom he found arms and ammunition hidden there.

"My room had *roshandans* (skylights to let the sun and air in) but no windows. The house was so sparsely furnished that I felt I would drown in the emptiness. I couldn't sleep at night because the walls seemed to scream fear, and anguish."

"The anger and fear of the earlier occupants probably permeated the walls of the house. I have heard that can happen. After all, our universe is one big sea of energy. Everything is connected," Amber replied.

"I agree and I'm so glad we moved to Delhi. I

like it here. This house is small, but it is new. We have great neighbors. At first, I missed the open spaces of Bhakkar, but I like it here now," said Aparna,

"I missed the quietness of Bhakkar when I first got married. When we moved to Shimla, I missed the activity of our life in Lahore." Amber smiled. "But now that I am used to the openness of Shimla, it is difficult to get used to all the people and the activity here in Delhi."

The three girls laughed, realizing that any change required adjustment. Aparna hugged Amber and Nina again.

"I'm so glad to see you both again."

***

After they had washed and freshened up, the family sat down for dinner. Amber's mother placed her hands on Amber's shoulders and bent to kiss her head. "I made your favorite dish, at least it used to be. I've made *kadi chawal*, rice with vegetable balls in a gram flour and yoghurt sauce.

"Yes, *Ammi*, I still love it," Amber replied.

"For you, my little *bitiya*," she said kissing Nina, I have made your favorite, *bharta*, roasted eggplant."

Nina laughed joyfully. "It is so good to be back with all of you."

Amber's mother smiled as she sat next to her at the head of the table. "Now that we are here together let us say a prayer of thanks to God who has kept us safe, and a prayer for dear Murad, may God always shower him with blessings." They closed their eyes to say a silent prayer.

116

"*Ammi*, your food is delicious," complimented Amber.

"Yes, *Nani*, this is the best *bharta* I have every tasted," added Nina.

Amber turned to her sister, "Aparna, I can't believe you are in you final year of college. What is your focus?"

"I'm in the Economics Honors program. After I graduate, I want to study law and work with Papa," replied Aparna. "Papa, yesterday, our teacher told us that India and Pakistan lost millions of rupees because of bank and shop closures, interrupted international trade and unharvested crops, so the government has added a refugee tax to recoup the losses. Is this going to raise prices?"

"This is not a new tax, but the government has increased it, this year. Yes, the prices have gone up. Freedom has its costs."

"But what exactly is the government doing to boost its economy?" Amber asked.

"The government has paid for the construction of schools, pharmacies, and houses. They are building factories. From an agricultural economy, we are shifting to an industrial one.

"The government has created job centers, employed refugees in work centers. They have cleared land in forested areas to make space for displaced accommodation. They've built training centers to teach women skills such as soap-making and embroidery, re-trained men as mechanics, carpenters, spinners, paper-makers, shoemakers."

***

117

Amber woke up the next morning to the comforting sound of the fan that clicked unceasingly overhead. She heard the sounds of the crows and sparrows outside. The milkman cycled past her window, singing. The sounds of hymns from a nearby temple came over a speaker. In spite of the noises, there was stillness. Amber felt a sense of peace. She glanced at the second bed to watch Nina sleeping.

Her mother heard Amber moving around, so she brought the tea tray into her room. The sight of the knitted tea cozy over the teapot sent a warm feeling over Amber. The tea smelled so good. It was delicious. Mrs. Vij brewed Darjeeling Orange Pekoe Pink, long leaf, along with a shorter leaf. The combination was heady.

"Oh Ma, I haven't had tea in bed for ages."

Her mother smiled. "I remembered our old times together. I would bring you tea, and we would sit on your bed and talk. Sometimes Aparna would wake up and join us."

"I loved that special time with you, Ma," Amber smiled as her mother poured the tea, milk and sugar in two cups.

"What would you like to do today?" her mother asked. "Your father will go to work soon, and Aparna will go to her college."

"I need to go to Grindlays Bank to deposit some money for Neil. Is there one close by?"

"There is one in Connaught Place, the main shopping center of New Delhi. It will take you twenty minutes by taxi," her mother replied.

"Okay, I think I will leave at 11 a.m. Nina will probably want to stay home with you. I will be back soon after I have completed the transaction. Where is Papa now?"

"He has gone for his morning walk. He likes to do that. It clears his head to begin a new day," her mother replied. "Aparna is getting ready to leave for college. I should get her breakfast ready. Do you want yours before you bathe?"

"No, I think I'll take a bath, then come for breakfast," replied Amber.

***

Amber was ready to leave for the bank when the phone rang. Amber answered. "Hello, this is the Vij residence."

"Amber, is that you?" It was Nayan.

"Yes. Nayan?"

"I'm in town for a couple of days. Can we meet today?"

"Sorry, I can't. I'm just leaving to go to Grindlays Bank. It's in Connaught Place. I don't know when I'll be back."

"I'm at the outer circle. I'll meet you at the bank in half an hour." He hung up.

***

Amber's taxi driver was a burly Sikh. He was tall, turbaned, and vociferous. He told Amber how he had migrated from Lahore, and when Amber told him that she was from the same city, he bonded with her and told her his whole life story. He did this while he tried to navigate through the mixed traffic. He shouted, blew the horn, his foot trembled over the accelerator, but everyone on the road seemed untroubled.

It was half an hour before the taxi reached the Georgian style, Connaught Place, which was named after the first Duke of Connaught, Queen Victoria's third son. It was a white circular two story complex with a manicured park in the center.

The taxi driver told Amber that Connaught Place was designed as three concentric circles creating an inner, middle, and outer circle. He dropped her off in front of the bank.

Nayan was waiting for her outside. He hugged her. "I've missed you so much. I couldn't wait to see you again." He walked into the bank with Amber and sat with her while she conducted her transaction.

After her work was done, Nayan asked her if she would have lunch with him.

"Oh no, I can't. I told *Ammi* I would come right back for lunch."

"Okay, at least let's have coffee. *Volgas* is close by. Let's go there," Nayan said, resigned. On the way a young shoeshine boy stopped them. "Sahib, please let me shine your shoes."

"Not today, son," Nayan told him as he urged Amber forward. He guided her through the colonnaded avenue, fronting the bank and stores towards B Block, to *Volgas*, but street vendors continually stopped them.

"These enterprising vendors or *patriwalas*, are Punjabi refugees," Nayan told her. "They buy at wholesale prices and sell items at throwaway prices. They are happy with a small profit, much to the chagrin of the larger shop owners of Connaught Place. You'll never see a single Punjabi refugee, begging for a handout. They have even started the cheaper *phat phatia* taxi-service. They use improvised four-seat vehicles which run on motor cycle engines discarded from the second world war."

Volgas was a lovely restaurant. The band played lively music. The ambience was welcoming. A polite waiter guided them to their table. They perused the menu and placed their orders.

Nayan held her hands. "You're in my mind all the time, Amber. I came to Delhi to attend some meetings, but I couldn't stop thinking of you. Of us. I'm in love with you, Amber. Please marry me, and we'll live happily ever after."

"There's no such thing as happily ever after," Amber said shaking her head. "There is no certainty in life."

"Stop this kind of thinking, please. I know you have feelings for me. Murad would understand. I promise that I'll never willingly leave you. Of course there is a risk that I could die. You will die too, one day, but that still gives us this day together. Will you never allow yourself to get close to anyone?" Nayan held her hands as she tried to pull away.

"Will you never allow yourself the joy of loving me, for fear that you might lose me? Will you deny us even this much happiness? To refuse to live fully, because one day you'll be gone, is senseless! If it had been you who had died instead of Murad, would you have wanted him to mourn you all his life?"

Put like that, it did sound ridiculous, but the heartaches of the past were a bitter lesson. She removed her hands from his. "If it were that simple, we wouldn't be arguing," Amber pointed out. "We met a just few months ago. How can I know if we are right for each other?"

"So, get to know me. We can have a long engagement. Our children will also come to understand us better. I'll know you have made a commitment to me."

"I'm not sure what you expect from a wife," Amber said.

Nayan clasped her hands. "I love you and I want you to love me and our children. In return, besides my love, you will have my respect, and admiration. I promise to take care of you, Neil, Nina, and Rowena and any other children we may or may not have. We can have a good life together. Say 'yes' Amber."

***

Amber knew that if Murad had still been in her life, she would have seen Nayan as just an attractive man who she could talk to easily. But Murad had not been in her life for over two years. She missed him. She'd been lonely too.

Should she embark on a new relationship? Nayan loved her, she knew, and she would make him a good wife. She loved Rowena. She liked Nayan very much. She would learn to love him as well. He was a strong, compassionate, and loving man. *Yes* was fluttering through her mind. Hope was taking wing, and Amber had no desire to tether it. She *would* take the steps forward to venture into what had to be a new world with Nayan. She didn't want to listen to the voices of caution anymore.

"Okay, yes," she said giving Nayan a brilliant smile. "Let me talk to my mother tonight."

The final decision would depend on several of her family members, but it was a relief to make a decision.

Nayan's smile was broad as he squeezed her hands. He took care of the bill. Neither of them had touched their coffee. "Let's get out of here, before you change your mind. I'll drive you home. You don't need to find a taxi. I'll get a chance to meet Nina again and also to meet your parents."

As they drove to Amber's home, Nayan asked, "Are you free for dinner tomorrow night? I don't leave until the day after. I'll be in meetings during the day, but I'd love to see you in the evening. Nina is welcome to come."

"I'm sorry. My friend Sheila has invited me to her house for dinner. I called Hari and Sheila this morning. She said they had invited guests over tomorrow and would love to have Nina and me join them. I agreed. I remember you said you knew Hari and Sheila too."

"I do. Hari invited me too, but I told him I was uncertain of my schedule. I wanted to touch base with you first. I will call Hari today to let him know I'll come. If you can't have dinner with me, at least I will see you there. I'll pick you both up from your house so you don't have to take a taxi." Nayan walked her to the door when they reached Amber's home. Amber's mother answered the bell. Amber introduced Nayan to her.

"Ma, this is Nayan Kapoor. His daughter studies at my school. Nayan's mother knows Murad's parents well. I met him at the bank today. He gave me a lift home."

Nayan bent to touch her feet. Her mother patted him on the head. "*Jitai raho,* live long. Please come in. You are just in time for lunch. Please stay."

Nayan was about to refuse when Amber's father walked in. The two men greeted each other politely.

123

"Papa, this is Nayan Kapoor from Shimla. He is a family friend. He is in Delhi for a few days."

Mr. Vij nodded. "Please come in. Stay for lunch. We are just about to have it."

"Thank you, but no. I should leave. I came in because my daughter wanted me to give a message to Nina," Nayan replied.

"You can give it to her over lunch. If you leave, I guarantee, you will miss out on one of the best meals you have ever had. My wife is an excellent cook." Mr. Vij smiled at his wife who gave him an admonishing look.

"He likes to exaggerate," his wife said affectionately, "but we won't send you away hungry."

Nayan relented. "I would love to stay to taste your delicious food and get to know you all as well."

"Amber, show Nayan where he can wash his hands and join us for lunch."

Nayan was walking back to the dining table when Nina walked out of her room.

"Uncle Nayan! What a surprise! Is Rowena with you?"

"Not this time. I will bring her, with my mother, to Delhi, in two weeks. She wants you to keep some time free for her," Nayan replied smiling.

"Of course," Nina replied. They all sat down for lunch. It was a simple meal and as predicted, absolutely delicious. Mrs. Vij had made *biryani*, rice with vegetables, and *raita*, yoghurt with cucumbers, tomatoes, salt, pepper, and cumin.

"Mrs. Vij, the food is delicious. Thank you for inviting me," Nayan said looking at Amber covertly. Amber was talking quietly to Nina.

"Didn't I tell you," Mr. Vij said proudly. "You will never taste a *biryani* like this. I never eat out. My taste buds have become too used to this, to appreciate some of the stuff they serve at five star restaurants." All of them nodded, smiling. The dessert was rice pudding with cardamoms and almonds. It was light, gently sweet, aromatic, and to die for.

Mr. Vij patted his stomach, satisfied. "This is why I married your beautiful mother," he said to Amber.

***

Nayan left after lunch, promising to pick up Nina and Amber the next evening to take them to Hari and Sheila's house.

"I was impressed by Nayan," Mr. Vij told his family. "The Kapoor chain of hotels is known for their elegance and efficiency. Nayan has turned them around single-handed. He has a good business head."

"Yes, I liked him, too," Mrs. Vij replied. "It is so sad that he is a widower. He must miss his wife. I feel sorry for his daughter as well. She must experience the void of not having her mother."

"I'm sure she does," said Nina, "but Rowena is a happy and lively young girl. She loves Mum and enjoys visiting with us."

"Well," said Mr. Vij standing up, "I enjoyed meeting the young man, and I enjoyed my lunch, but now I must return to work. I will see you all in the evening."

Hari and Sheila's Dinner
The next evening Nina asked Amber if it would be all right if she did not accompany Amber to her friends' house.

"I'd rather spend time with Aparna. I think she can help me decide what I should focus on in college next year. I have always wanted to be a doctor, but Aparna feels that I should pursue my love of music and painting. Aparna thinks I have great talent."

"You can do both. Medicine will provide you with the satisfaction of helping your community, and the arts will allow your creative talents to be nurtured. You have a year to decide, but stay at home if that is what you want."

The doorbell rang and Aparna went to answer it. She smiled at Nayan. "Come in. You must be Nayan. Amber told me you were coming."

"You must be Aparna. Amber has talked about you. Nina looks up to you so much. Are the two ready?" Nayan asked smiling.

"Amber is ready. Nina wanted to spend time with me tonight."

At that moment Amber and Nina walked out to greet Nayan.

"Hi, Uncle Nayan."

"I hear you are not coming tonight."

"I am afraid not. I need to spend some time with Aparna. I am sure Uncle Hari and Aunty Sheila won't mind," Nina replied.

***

The hosts lived on the ground floor of the Palace of Jind. Many of the palaces had been ceded to the Indian government and were used as government housing. A long driveway, with sprawling gardens on each side, led to house. Nayan and Amber walked up the steps to a large covered veranda leading to the front door.

Hari and Sheila were delighted to see them. Sheila gave Amber a long hug.

"Hari and I were saddened and shocked by the news about Murad. I am so sorry, Amber. This senseless partition has taken too many lives," she said teary-eyed.

"I hated to leave Lahore," Sheila continued. "But now, in hindsight, I'm glad we moved in 1946. The partition in 1947 brought so much chaos and destruction. When we first moved to New Delhi, it was just a quiet, colonial suburb of the old city. I missed my Lahore so much. Don't get me wrong. New Delhi is beautiful. Edward Lutyens planned the new city well. The government buildings are grand. The broad avenues, parks, fountains all add to its beauty. I just miss my friends."

Amber nodded sympathetically, even though it was difficult to feel sorry for Sheila, who was happy and safe with her family.

Hari gave Amber a hug as well. "I'm so sorry, Amber. I was shocked to hear the news. Murad was my best friend. I just wish he had listened to me when I told him to move to New Delhi in 1947."

"Come," said Sheila. "Let me introduce you to the other guests. Meet Iqbal and Rajinder Aluwalia. They are Hari's relatives from Sialkot who are staying with us till they can find a house. They moved to New Delhi, last year. And these are our friends, Steve and Martha Gonzales, Danyal and Gulab Ginwala, and Iqbal Ali Akhtar."

To her friends she said, "Meet Nayan Kapoor and Amber Mehra. Amber is visiting from Shimla, and

127

Nayan has just flown in from Bombay. I'm so glad we could all get together!"

Nayan laughed as he listened to the last names of the guests. "We have Sikhs, Christians, Parsis, Hindus and a Muslim right here in this room. A truly united India. What do we need politicians for?"

They all laughed with Nayan as the new arrivals were seated. There was such warmth and camaraderie in the room, Amber felt very welcome.

"Nayan, what can I offer you to drink?" Hari asked.

"I'll have a scotch on the rocks."

"A *Johnny Walker* coming up. Amber?"

"Do you have any juice?" Amber asked.

"We have orange, pineapple, mango and guava juice."

"I'll try the mango," Amber replied.

Amber turned to Sheila. "Where are the children? They must have grown so much by now."

"Yes, Satish is fourteen, Asha is seven, and Rohini, the baby, is three. The older two are doing their homework. The baby is asleep. Satish and Asha will have dinner with us," Sheila replied. "Tell me about Nina and Neil. I was looking forward to seeing Nina today."

"I'm sorry, I'll bring her over soon. Nina is seventeen. She will graduate next year. Neil is twenty. He is at Oxford. He is studying economics and finance.

"After we moved to Shimla, I wanted Neil to study in India. But our friend, Howard Skinner insisted on taking Neil with him to England where Neil had admission at a college in Cambridge. I was so devastated at that time, I was glad to leave Howard in

128

charge of Neil. He actually helped Neil get a scholarship at another college in Oxford. So Neil switched colleges and he is happy there. The college seems like a good fit for him. I am thankful to Howard."

"Are you and Nina happy living with Murad's parents?" Sheila asked, concerned.

"Yes. I was offered a cottage on the Loreto Convent grounds, but I knew if we moved, it would break *Ammi* and Papa's heart. This is not a permanent solution, but for now I feel I am doing the right thing," Amber explained.

"Maybe one day you will consider marrying again, even though I know Murad was the love of your life." She glanced at Nayan.

Amber did not answer.

"Hari, you are in charge of rehabilitating refugees. Have you been successful?" Danyal asked.

"For the most part. There were some delays because we were required to check if the refugees had land or housing in Pakistan before we could give them their share. The ones who came with proof, were the first to be resettled. We were lucky that New Delhi had huge tracts of undeveloped land to the south and west of the city. We built resettlement colonies as fast as we could. The capital has expanded to twice its original size."

"What about the people who had nothing?" asked Iqbal.

"We have provided jobs for them and they can rent a place in the new housing settlements."

"My father told me you helped him find housing for many of his clients. Thank you," Amber said gratefully. "The refugees have made so many sacrifices."

129

"I did the best I could. Most of the refugees now have jobs and housing."

"There are some refugees that seem homeless and jobless. There were a few sitting on the pavement, in front of my house, yesterday," contradicted Martha. "Occasionally they shouted, '*Hindustan Zindabad! Musalmano, koh nikalo,*' Long live India, remove the Muslims. Finding no Muslims in our neighborhood, they seemed at a loss for what to do next. I told them to leave us innocent people alone. They continued to sit there and smoke their *beedis* (cigarettes). When they heard a shout from the next street, they charged into action, running towards the sound."

"They might be new migrants, not the refugees from Punjab," explained Nayan.

***

The influx of the first Punjabi refugees was soon followed by migrations from the rural areas of North India. Landless farmers and villagers came down in search of jobs. Driven by economic need rather than religious struggles, these new arrivals had to compete with the refugees. When they didn't find jobs right away, they found causes to stay active. The politicians cleverly put forward the cause of 'hatred' towards religions other than Hinduism.

***

"It's too bad the politicians are not doing their share to foster unity. I always thought New Delhi also meant new hope," murmured Gulab Ginwala. "Iqbal, you have stayed back in India, even though you are a Muslim. Do you feel safe here?" she asked.

Iqbal shrugged. "I'm a bachelor. I grew up in the old city. I own three book shops there. I know all the residents in my area. They are my family. I have some family members in Pakistan but I am not in touch with them. Do I feel safe here? I think so. Those who don't know me, sometimes look at me with suspicion. But I also have good friends. My parents gave me the name *Iqbal*. It could be Muslim, Hindu or a Sikh name. Look at brother Iqbal Aluwalia. He is Sikh, but we are bound by our common name. Names are derived from language not religion."

Iqbal Aluwalia nodded in agreement. "When I was growing up in the 1920s in Sialkot, a very small percentage moved out of the state or province of their birth. We didn't question religion. We had deep-rooted social and cultural bonds. We depended on each other and learned to live with one another. All this was soon forgotten or ignored in the fervor of separatist rhetoric. People seemed to forget the voice of reason in favor of bigotry and intolerance as they crossed borders."

"Delhi has provided exiled Punjabis another place to call home," murmured his wife, Rajinder. "I am grateful for that."

The housekeeper announced that the dinner was on the table so the guests rose to take their conversations to the other room.

Hari introduced his son and daughter who joined them for dinner. There was a tone of affection and pride in his voice.

As they drove to Amber's house, Nayan asked Amber if she had enjoyed her evening.

"Yes, it was great to meet so many people from different religions and cultures and yet we had so much in common. We are all survivors to some extent," Amber replied. "We had to move from our original homes to make new homes for ourselves."

"It was interesting to hear Iqbal Ali's thoughts on his life here in Delhi after the partition. I know it must not be easy. Politicians make sure that the hostilities among different groups stay alive. It suits their purpose."

Amber sighed. Nayan put his arm around her shoulders.

"Did you get a chance to talk to your parents about us?"

Amber shook her head.

"Don't worry. I'll bring my mother and Rowena soon. Your parents will get a chance to know them as well. Maybe you should talk to them after they all meet."

***

"Nina, while we are in Delhi, I'd like us to shop for you. You haven't done much in Shimla. You need coats, boots, sweaters, and a few new outfits. Would you like to shop today?" Amber asked Nina.

"Yes, let's," Aparna interrupted. "Today is my first day off. Our college is officially closed for the winter and I can't wait to celebrate. *Ammi* wanted to buy some *Kohlapuri chappals* from Queen's Way. Those leather slippers from Kohlapur are the only kind that last. I'll ask her to join us. The four of us can make it a ladies' day of shopping! Let's leave right after breakfast."

"Okay, okay, I'll be ready," said Nina resigned. She would rather have read a book, but when Aparna reminded her there were three bookshops at the Queen's Way shopping center, she brightened.

"Where is Queen's Way? Is it close to Connaught Place?" Amber asked.

"Yes, it's a road that starts at Connaught Place and runs north-south all the way to King's Way and Windsor Place. The market itself is a kilometer-and-a-half stretch lined with boutique stores and refugee footpath hawkers from Punjab and Bengal. You can buy clothes, shoes, handicrafts, silver and costume jewelry, books, magazines, and fast food, at budget prices. You'll never see the variety available at Queen's Way in any of the large, snobby stores of Connaught Place."

The four women hailed a four-seater *phat phatia* to take them to the shopping bazaar. The *phat phatia* driver jump-started his motorcycle. *Br-a-a-amph, phat phat phat*, he twisted the throttle more than was needed. They lurched forward with a surprising burst of speed and the rickshaw raced towards its destination. The women clutched at their seats as the wind blew their hair and the loud *phat phat* of the motorcycle drowned any other sounds. Suddenly the vehicle swerved to avoid a pedestrian who decided to walk in front of their vehicle with casual confidence. Amber leaned over to stop Nina from falling forward.

"Slow down, please!" Amber's mother yelled at the driver. The driver raced on blasting his horn continuously as they bounced and teetered over potholes like drunk sailors. He braked suddenly as they reached their destination nearly tossing out the passengers. Out of breath and hearts beating fast, they paid the driver.

"No wonder these rickshaws are much cheaper than the black and yellow taxis. There is no guarantee we'll get out of the experience alive!" Nina gasped.

"Oh come on. Admit it. It was exciting. You didn't even have to pay extra for the roller coaster ride," Aparna said, laughing.

"It was a hair-raising ride!"

"You look cute, just windblown, and a rickshaw ride is a great way to attain Nirvana," Aparna replied, sliding her arm through Nina's. "Let's shop."

"These stores are like the kiosks we have at the Lakkar Bazaar in Shimla. There are so many people. Look at all the colorful handicrafts!" Nina exclaimed.

The four women window-shopped for a while as they peered into each store while footpath hawkers tried to attract them to buy their wares.

They stopped at a shop selling colorful skirts, T-shirts, and handbags. Both Aparna and Nina bought a skirt, a top, and, matching totes. Amber's mother found her *chappals* at the shoe store.

"Nina, you need boots and a coat, some woolen slacks, and a jacket," Amber reminded her daughter. A few hours later, they had all found what they needed. Amber was the only one who had not bought anything for herself, but she was exhausted from all the bargaining she had done.

"I'm so tired, I could sit right here on the pavement!" Amber's mother gasped.

Amber placed an arm around her mother. "I'll find us a place to eat."

There was a snack bar close by so they headed in that direction. Everyone was glad to sit as they laid the purchases on the floor beside them. The menus were large with a plastic laminate.

"Why don't we order four dishes?" Amber suggested. "We can share."

They agreed. "Do all of you like cheese *pakoras*, fritters, *chole bhatura*, spiced garbanzos with bread, *idli* and *sambhar*, steamed rice cakes with a dipping soup, any other suggestions?"

"I think there is more than enough food for us already," said Amber's mother. "If we need more, we'll order it later. Don't forget, we also have dinner ready at home."

As the four walked out of the snack bar, Nina spotted a taxi stand on the right. On a full stomach, laden with packages, they didn't want to risk their lives, or their shopping, on the rickshaw, so a taxi was very welcome. Unfortunately, the taxi driver was nearly as crazy as the *Phat Phatia-wala* who had brought them to the market.

"Who has right of way?" Nina asked under her breath.

Aparna grinned. "Traffic entering the road from the left has priority. Also traffic from the right, and traffic from the middle. But the cow takes precedence over all other traffic. Everyone must slow down for the cow. Just close your eyes. Don't worry."

Their driver presumed it was essential to overtake every car. He honked his horn and passed. Unperturbed, the driver who he passed, blew his horn louder and overtook their taxi driver. Everyone on the road honked. Suddenly their taxi driver gave five honks, and waved. He had recognized someone he knew. The ride home was a hallucinatory potion of sound, sometimes hilarious, but also fun. They scrambled out, as the housekeeper rushed out to help them with their packages.

"There are visitors inside," he said. "They are having tea with Vij Sahib."

"Who are they?"

"One of them is Nayan Sahib. I don't know who are the other two."

"Maybe they are Nayan's mother and his daughter, Rowena. Nayan did say he would bring them," Amber mused.

They walked into the house to find Rowena sitting happily on Mr. Vij's lap. Nayan and Mrs. Kapoor were sitting across. Rowena scrambled down from her perch.

"Miss Amber, Nina!" She gave them hugs, and then looked shyly at Mrs. Vij and Aparna. Amber kneeled down to kiss Rowena's forehead.

"How are you my little one?"

"We reached here yesterday, and this morning, *Dadi* took me to my old school to visit my teachers and meet some of my friends. Mother Superior remembered me. She told me she missed me. I played with my friends during recess. *Dadi* bought each of my friends, a piece of chocolate fudge, erasures, and pencils from our *trunkwala*, who sells them."

Nayan stood up, smiling, as he watched his daughter chatter. "I'm sorry, I couldn't call ahead. The phone lines were down and Rowena was too impatient," Nayan apologized.

"Never mind," smiled Amber's mother. "I am very happy you are here. I am only sorry we weren't here to welcome you. Sit down, and I will get some more tea."

"We actually came to invite you to our house for lunch this Sunday. I hope you'll all come," invited Mrs. Kapoor.

Mrs. Vij looked at her husband. He nodded.

"We'd love to. Maybe I can bring a dish."

"No, no. It will be a simple meal. I can handle it," Mrs. Kapoor replied.

Amber's mother took the empty pot to the kitchen to refill it with fresh tealeaves and boiling water. *There's nothing like a hot cup of tea on a cold day*, she thought.

***

"I've arranged to borrow a van and driver from our neighbor," said Mr. Vij, "I want to take you all to see the Taj Mahal in Agra. It will be a three-hour journey, but none of us has been there, so I am sure it will be a good experience. Let's pack a picnic lunch, on Friday, and we can eat on the grounds of the Taj. I don't know if you are free, Nayan, but Mrs. Kapoor and Rowena are welcome to join us," Mr. Vij said.

"I want to go!" Rowena exclaimed. "Papa, can't you take Friday off?"

"Yes," his mother urged, "take the day off. You need some time away from your work."

"Is there enough room in the van?" Nayan asked.

Mr. Vij nodded. "I believe it seats ten. It's settled. You'll all come."

Everybody smiled at Rowena as she yelled, "Yea!"

"I'm doing this for us. I want to spend time with you," Nayan whispered in Amber's ear before he left.

***

As they approached Agra city, they tried to spot the large white marble dome in the distance. They went over a bridge across the river Jamuna to reach Agra. Lining the river were Hindu shrines and temples, with brightly painted idols of Hanuman, the monkey god, and *Kali Devi*, the destroyer of evil forces. Her eight arms spread out as she danced over her consort, the prostrate, Lord Shiva.

As they approached the white, marble building, Mr. Vij took Rowena's hand. "This is the Taj Mahal. In the 1600s, Emperor Shah Jahan built this mausoleum in memory of his wife, Mumtaz Mahal. It is constructed of white marble, inlaid with semi-precious stones. Its central dome is 240-feet high. It is surrounded by four smaller domes, while four minarets stand at the corners."

"May we go inside?" Rowena asked eagerly.

They had to take off their shoes, and cover their heads, to enter. On the walls of the central chamber were inlaid flowers. Verses from the Quran were inscribed on the arched entrances to the mausoleum. Inside the mausoleum, an octagonal marble chamber, adorned with carvings and precious stones, housed the cenotaph, the false tomb of Mumtaz. The real sarcophagus with her ashes lay below at garden level.

Rowena had to be rushed out of the dark tomb that smelled of incense and perspiration. She felt suffocated. Amber climbed back with her.

Rowena and Amber enjoyed climbing the minarets. They ran up the spiral staircase and stepped

138

out on to the circular balcony where they saw the gardens spread out below, with fountains and reflecting pools.

"We'll picnic there," Amber said pointing to the gardens next to the pools. In the opposite direction she pointed out the River Jamuna and the Red Fort that lay beyond. The emperor Aurangzeb had imprisoned his father, Shah Jahan in this fort.

They all met outside and laid out a blanket for their picnic lunch. It was fun. Eagles and crows hovered nearby waiting for any leftovers. Monkeys and squirrels also lived in the gardens. They came up boldly to beg for food. Nayan, sitting next to Amber, whispered in her ear.

"I wish we were together right now. Just you and me."

Amber squeezed his hand. "Sh-h. You can be heard."

"I don't care. I want you with me."

"You know," said Mr. Vij, turning towards them, "the Mughals and the British ignored the Taj until the end of the 19th century. Lord Curzon ordered a restoration of the Taj that got completed in 1908, but most of the original jewels were removed and sent to England."

"The British took most of the jewels from the Indian treasury," commented Mrs. Kapoor. "They have our 105-carat diamond, the Kohinoor, as well."

***

After visiting Agra, they drove on to Fatehpur Sikri, a Mughal city built by Akbar. Wandering around the empty sandstone structures, they tried to imagine what it was like when the emperor was alive. There was a giant Parchisi board.

"Dancing girls or royal servants were used as gaming pieces," they heard a tour guide tell a group of tourists. "Parchisi originated in India in the 6th century. There is depiction of these boards in the Ajanta caves. The British borrowed the idea of this game. They modified it by introducing a single six-sided dice, called it Ludo, and patented it in 1896."

The guide showed them iron rings on the ground where elephants were tethered. "Condemned prisoners are said to have been crushed to death under the elephants' feet," he told the horrified tourists.

Inside the walls of Fatehpur Sikri was an abandoned mosque, which faced west towards Mecca. The walls were bare except for a few geometric patterns carved into the stone. A short distance from the mosque lay the tomb of the Sufi saint, Sheikh Salim Chishti, who inspired Akbar to start his own religion, *Din Illahi*, a combination of Christianity, Islam, and Hinduism.

On the return journey, Nayan sat next to Amber. His daughter sat on the other side. Rowena snuggled up against him. Nayan put one arm around her and the other around Amber.

"At last," he whispered. "This trip wasn't as I had pictured. I had thought we would have time to talk, but with so many of us, it was difficult."

"I know."

They sat together companionably. Rowena's head had slipped to his lap. She was tired. Nayan stroked his daughter's hair.

His affection for his daughter was beautiful to watch. Amber felt a lump form in her throat at the sight.

140

"She's asleep already," he whispered looking at Amber. He nudged Amber closer to him. She couldn't help being aware of his muscled body against her own, and the smell of his mild after-shave.

***

Nayan and his mother sat in his large veranda drinking their morning tea. They had woken up that morning to a black morning sky. It would rain soon. They could hear thunder in the distance.

"If it rains, I hope it stops before lunch. The Vij's and Amber might find it difficult to get a taxi in bad weather," Mrs. Kapoor commented.

"Don't worry, Ma, if that happens, I'll pick them up," Nayan replied. He looked out at his lush green lawns spread before his bungalow. He hoped Amber would like his home. Nayan's two-story home contained four master suites. The living room was large enough to entertain at least fifty people. His front lawns could accommodate many more guests. He needed to entertain more. Lately he'd been too busy.

"You have invited four other guests haven't you?" Nayan's mother asked.

"I invited Hari and Sheila, but they can't come because one of their children is sick. I've invited Chander and his wife, Sugni. I have also invited Balwant Singh and Ashok Dutt. You've met them all. I just feel bad I haven't invited them sooner but being on my own, I just didn't feel like entertaining."

Mrs. Kapoor nodded. "What you need is a wife to help you."

The first few drops were huge. They splashed into the veranda with the intensity of hail. The clouds clashed in the sky with earth shattering thunder. Fat raindrops fought their way through the thick air and fell on the ground below.

"It's like watching an ocean pouring through a sieve," said Mrs. Kapoor, shaking her head. "I'd better check on Rowena. She is sleeping, but she might wake up scared by the sound of thunder. It's getting very cold outside."

"I'll come in with you," said Nayan gathering up the teapot and cups.

"If you are coming in, then check on Rowena. I will see if Ramu has finished chopping the vegetables that I need to cook for our lunch."

"Would you rather I hired a permanent cook, Ma? Ramu is rather young and helps you only part-time," Nayan asked his mother.

"No, no. That won't be necessary."

Nayan's Lunch, New Delhi
When Amber and her family reached Nayan's house, the sun was pushing its way through the clouds. It had stopped raining. Mrs. Kapoor and Nayan welcomed them warmly and Nayan introduced them to the other guests. "This is Chander Rai, and his wife Sugni. Chander is my lawyer. He takes care of all the legal work involved with my hotels. This is Ashok Dutt. He makes sure we are all safe. He is a police chief," said Nayan grinning. "Balwant Singh works at the Department of Rehabilitation." He went on to introducing Amber's family to the rest of the guests.

Mr. Vij recognized Balwant immediately from the zealous work he was doing to bring back abducted women from across the border. He was surprised to learn, however, that among the women abducted, and not returned, was Balwant Singh's own wife, Simran. Mr. Singh was a tall distinguished looking gentleman of about thirty-five. But grief was etched into his face.

Rowena stood quietly to one side. With all these new faces, she had turned suddenly shy.

"Let's go to my room for a while," she whispered to Nina. Aparna and Nina followed Rowena.

Ramu brought soft drinks for everyone and Mrs. Kapoor passed around vegetable fritters and nuts. Later the cook returned with freshly fried samosas, triangular shaped pastries, stuffed with potatoes, peas, and onions. The guests ate them with a cilantro and mint sauce.

"I have heard that bringing the women back to their country is not easy," Sugni said to Balwant Singh.

"We have used subterfuge and disguise. Many women are employed in the rescue. They seem to be better placed to handle the situation and to persuade those women who are reluctant to give up their new homes. Some have children by Muslim fathers. They feel they will not be accepted back by their families," Balwant replied.

"They ask why they should go to India. They would only be accused of practicing Islam and of being unchaste or impure."

Mr. Vij nodded. "The two countries have agreed, in principle, to work together and keep their borders open to the rescue teams. Such openness is not always possible. People in positions of authority made many of the abductions. In many instances, the police themselves were the culprits. This happened on both sides."

Ashok Dutt agreed. "We have tried to remove the corruption, but at the time of the partition, we lost

143

control. In one instance, two assistant sub-inspectors of police went to recover an abducted woman and then raped her.

"Mridula Sarabhai has done a great job of working with all departments and has brought truckloads of women back to India. She is in charge of the Central Recovery Operation. She has brought hundreds of women back to their homes."

Balwant Singh's voice rose. "What makes me really angry is when these abducted women are returned, some husbands and families refuse to have anything to do with them. They call them impure and sluts. They ask, why they didn't take poison and preserve their virtue and their honor? This is a hard-hearted world in which many husbands refuse to acknowledge their wives. If only my Simran could be found, I know I will honor her with my heart and soul!"

Everyone was stunned by the fervor in Singh's voice. Ashok patted his shoulder, sympathetically. "Don't lose hope, Balwant. Simran will return. Every day, more and more women are returning."

Lunch was served, and the guests moved to the dining room. Rowena, Nina, and Aparna joined the guests.

"I showed Nina and Aparna our house," Rowena told Nayan. "They liked it."

Nayan smiled at his daughter. "Great."

The lunch was delicious, and the talk was more general now. The tension eased.

Mrs. Kapoor brought the desserts out on the lawn where the sun shone welcomingly. Raindrops sparkled on the leaves and flowers. Ramu had spread a *duree,* or cotton rug, over the damp grass, under the lawn chairs.

After finishing their desserts, Mr. Vij and Chander Rai closed their eyes. The sun felt good on their faces. Sugni sighed and rose from her chair, "I think we had better leave before we all fall asleep here. The lunch was so good, but that delicious food has made me lazy. And I can see Chander is ready for his afternoon nap.

Balwant and Ashok stood up as well. "Yes, we should make a move."

"Don't all of you leave at the same time!" Mrs. Kapoor protested. She looked at Mrs. Vij and said, "You'll stay a little longer won't you? Have tea at least. You promised to share with me your recipe for *Biryani.*"

Nayan agreed. "Yes, stay for a while longer." He walked Balwant, Ashok and the Rais' to their cars and returned to join the rest.

Rowena was excited as she turned to Nayan. "Papa, may I show Nina and Aparna the peacocks in the Rose Gardens nearby. We'll be back soon. The peacocks are beautiful and they love to show off their wing span of colors."

"Only if Aparna and Nina want to see them," Nayan told her.

It was agreed. The girls walked down the street towards the public gardens. Mrs. Kapoor asked Ramu to make tea for them. The women talked animatedly. Mr. Vij let out a soft snore. Sleep had overtaken him.

Nayan nudged Amber lightly. Aloud, he said, "Let me show you around the house while our mothers talk."

"Go, look around," Mrs. Kapoor encouraged. "Amber, your mother is sharing some of her best recipes with me."

Amber followed Nayan in. "You have a lovely house."

"I agree." He placed his arm around her shoulders. "Though all I care about right now is that we are alone at last. We can forget the rest of the world for a while. You make me come alive, Amber."

He turned to her. His mouth touched her cheek, his lips cool and firm. Then his lips moved to her mouth, stunning her because Nayan had never kissed her before.

She tried to move away. "Ramu might walk in with the tea service," she whispered. Nayan lifted his head for a moment and lead them into another room where they wouldn't be disturbed. He kissed her again.

It was a searching kiss. It wasn't a deep, passionate kiss, nor was it one of mere friendliness. It was somewhere in between, warm and slow, filling Amber's heart with a hint of promise. It was a kiss of exploration, a kiss of – expectation.

She tried to pull away, but his hand curled around the back of her head, his thumb tilting her chin. For one surprised second her eyes stared into his, warm and alive, twinkling with topaz depths. He sighed and smiled and reluctantly released her.

"Okay, let's make this tour of my house authentic." He took her hand to guide her in. The inside of Nayan's house was a sea of mosaic and marble. She had already seen the intimate drawing room where elegant couches and armchairs encircled a large hand-knotted Persian rug in shades of red, ochre and gold.

146

She had not seen the bedroom suites on the second floor. Each suite had a bedroom with a sitting area. They opened to a wide balcony overlooking the landscaped gardens where they had sat earlier and where the mothers conversed. The fragrance of honeysuckle drifted to the balcony.

"What an amazing view. It's like your own private paradise on earth. I hope you get to share it with your friends. It would be a crime not to."

"Unfortunately, I haven't had much time to invite friends lately. I'm not here very often. And even when I am, I am too busy taking care of the business and Rowena. I really don't have time to entertain."

"It must have been difficult for you after your wife and your father died."

"Yes, it was." Then he glanced up and asked Amber to look at the sky.

Amber looked up and saw one of the most breathtaking displays of natural beauty. The sun's dazzling globe had angled and dipped. Its sienna rays bled hauntingly into the dark blue sky. Nature was impervious to massacres, abductions, killings, and grief. Amber breathed deeply. This natural beauty is what had helped her survive the imperfections of human nature during the partition.

She turned to Nayan with a dimpled smile. "God's miracle!"

He looked at her, transfixed. The more he was in Amber's refreshing company, the more her beauty and intelligence enthralled him.

***

The next morning Amber stood in the kitchen brewing tea with her mother. It rained steadily but not with the ferocity of yesterday's rainfall. The temperature had dropped to 45 degrees Fahrenheit. Amber pulled her woolen robe around tighter and shivered slightly.

"Let's take our tea into the dining room. The electric heater is already switched on. That room will be warmer," said Mrs. Vij. Amber took the teapot and cups on a tray to the next room. Mrs. Vij brought a plate of cake rusks and a decorative round box to the table.

"I love dipping cake rusks in my tea. The cardamom flavor is so good," sighed Amber. Mrs. Vij opened the lid of the round box. Inside nestled a homemade fruitcake that smelled mouthwateringly of cloves, cinnamon and nutmeg.

"Did you make this?"

"No. Our neighbor, Gladys, brought it over. She marinates her fruit in brandy and other juices, for a month before she bakes it. Her cakes are always delicious.

She brought us plum pudding for Christmas. She is Anglo-Indian and a staunch Christian. On December 25th, her sons and daughters, with their families, came for Christmas brunch. She invited us too," said Mrs. Vij smiling as she thought fondly of her friend and neighbor. Gladys had helped her so much when she had first moved to Delhi.

"Amber," her mother voiced tentatively. "We have never talked about what you went through when you got the news that Murad was missing. You have been so strong for Nina and Neil. I know you still live with Murad's parents, but you are independent. You have a good job."

"It was difficult at first, Ma. But I didn't have much time to grieve. *Ammi* and Papa were shattered.

Murad was their only son. I had to take care of them. I also needed to care for Nina. She had moved to a new town, changed schools, just lost a father and even her brother had just left to study in England. I had a new job. I had to learn to take charge of my life fast."

Mrs. Vij smiled sadly. "This partition has caused so many losses. It is difficult to imagine a holocaust like this, let alone live through it." She clasped Amber's hands. "Have you ever thought of your future?"

"What do you mean?"

"Have you thought of marrying again?"

Amber looked at her surprised. "What brought this thought up suddenly?"

"Mrs. Kapoor brought it up. Your papa and I have worried about this too. Nayan's mother thinks you and he are a good match, and I think so too. I can see he admires you, and Rowena adores you. You like Nayan too, don't you?"

Amber was stunned. "Mrs. Kapoor talked to you? Does Nayan know?"

"I don't know if he knows or not, but you haven't answered my question. Do you like Nayan?"

"Yes, I like Nayan, Ma. But I don't know what *Ammi* and papa and Neil would think about me marrying again," replied Amber. "I don't want to hurt them. They mean a lot to me."

"Neil is a grown boy. After he returns from England, he will leave you to find work. He will get married. Nina will want to marry one day. Have you ever thought how difficult it will be for her to find a suitable match when she does not have a father?

149

"This is India. Life is not easy for widows and their children. Widowers get married again to young women, but it is not the same for widows."

"Ma, I know Nayan will make a good husband," Amber replied. "He is thoughtful, respectful, and he says he loves me."

"Don't wait, Amber. Any girl should be proud to be Nayan's wife. He is good looking, he respects his elders, he dotes on his daughter, and he is very rich."

"I have to get the approval of Murad's parents. I won't hurt them. They have done so much for me." Amber replied.

"They approve. I talked to them on the day after you left Shimla to come to Delhi. We had booked a call to check if you and Nina had boarded your train. They told me about the conversation they had with Mrs. Kapoor. They love you, Amber, and they miss Murad, but they feel you should move on. Neil and Nina need a father. We are all aging. We will not be alive forever. We will leave you, but you don't need to live alone."

Amber shook her head in despair. "Everyone knows, and I thought I would talk about this when I felt it was the right time."

"It is the right time, Amber," Mrs. Vij said in a firm voice. She clasped Amber's hands in her own. Nayan is a good man. I have faith in your goodness too. You will love and care for Rowena like she is your own. Nina likes and admires Nayan. We all like him.

"People talk you know. When you are a widow, even women can be callous. Nayan has the power and the money to stop tongues from wagging. You are a good woman, Amber. I am sorry about Murad, but you deserve to find happiness again. He loved you. He would not want you to stay single and lonely for the rest of your life."

Amber nodded her head. "That's what Nayan said. Okay, I will accept Nayan's hand in marriage, but I will not marry Nayan until Neil has met him.

***

A flurry of stormy wind crashed against the windows. Nina hated this weather and snuggled deeper into her covers.

"Move over, sleepy head," Aparna giggled in Nina's ear. "I'm freezing in my bed. My hot water bottle is like ice now. I need your warm body to snuggle up to."

"Leave me alone," Nina mumbled.

"Be a sport," Aparna pleaded. Nina edged over to leave her some space to crawl into her bed. Then she screamed.

"Aparna, you are like an icicle!"

Aparna giggled and just snuggled up to her niece. "Did you hear the rain all night?"

"I hate this weather," Nina grumbled.

"*Ammi* is making a special rainy day breakfast for us, complete with *pooras*, sweet semolina pancakes, and *halwa*. After breakfast we can sit in front of our heater and read books or just talk."

"Umm, nice!"

"Hey, do you think your Uncle Nayan likes my sister?"

"Un huh."

"Does that mean, he does?"

"Un huh."

"I knew it. I noticed how he sends tender glances her way, when he thinks nobody is looking," whispered Aparna conspiratorially.

Nina giggled.

"Do you like your Uncle Nayan?

"Mm. I like him."

"Would you object if your mother and Uncle Nayan got together?"

"I don't know. I don't think so. I think *Ammi* is lonely sometimes. Many nights I have heard her cry herself to sleep. I think she misses Papa but never talks about it. She feels she has to be strong for all of us."

"Maybe we should help them?" Aparna asked.

"I don't think that will be necessary," Nina replied dryly. "They are both adults. They are old enough to talk to each other frankly."

***

Amber's parents talked to Mr. and Mrs. Mehra. Murad's parents wanted to talk directly with Amber. They were happy to give their approval. Amber had spoken to Nina and Aparna earlier. They said they thought this was for the best.

Nayan was delighted and Rowena was ecstatic. It was decided Amber and Nayan would have a *roka* ceremony. Among Punjabis this was a simple event that takes place before the engagement. Amber and Murad had skipped this event because of the shortage of time. It was the step before the actual engagement. '*Rok*' meant 'stop.'

Nayan's mother explained to him that with a '*roka*' families of the bride and groom announce they have stopped looking for a match for their daughter or son. "A *roka* is not as formal as an engagement."

"I wish we could just get married tomorrow," Nayan complained.

Mr. and Mrs. Vij, along with Aparna, and Nina took *shagan* of sweets, gifts, and money. Nayan was surprised when he didn't see Amber. He had looked forward to seeing her. So had Rowena. She was so excited when she realized that Miss Amber would be her mother. He went to the next room when there was a break in the ceremony. He called Amber.

"Where are you? You should have been here. I miss you! What kind of ceremony is this where the bride-to-be is missing?"

"That's the custom. *Ammi* and Papa want to do this right," Amber replied. "But I'll be thinking of you and picturing the ceremony."

"Don't worry about that, I'll give you a step-by-step account."

Amber smiled. "I'd like that."

A priest had been invited to say prayers to bless this alliance. Nayan sat on the floor cross-legged facing the priest. Mr. and Mrs. Vij sat on the right of the priest and Mrs. Kapoor sat on the left. Rowena, Nina and Aparna sat behind Nayan.

Rowena clung to Nina, awestruck by this sacred ceremony. She couldn't believe Miss Amber was going to be her mother and Nina, her sister. She loved them both so much.

The prayer ended with the *tilak* ceremony where the priest applied a paste of sandalwood, rice grains, and saffron on Nayan's forehead. Mr. and Mrs. Vij offered sweets to Nayan, and the whole family. The priest congratulated Nayan. Both the families exchanged boxes of sweets, dry fruit, and baskets of fresh fruit.

Amber's parents gave a gold coin, and clothes for Nayan, Rowena, and Mrs. Kapoor.

Nayan's mother gave a *chunni*, a sheer head covering, along with a gold necklace, ear rings and a ring for Amber and a *salwar kameez*, the traditional Punjabi dress, for Nina.

The priest was offered lunch and, as a sign of respect, only after he had competed his meal and taken his leave, was lunch served to the rest of the guests.

"Papa, is Miss Amber really going to be my mommy?" Rowena asked.

Nayan nodded giving her a hug. She then turned to Nina. "And you will be my big sister?"

Nina hugged her. "Yes, Rowena. I'll be your big sister, so you'll have to listen to me."

"I'm so happy!" Rowena grinned. "This is the best day of my life."

***

The *roka* ceremony was the start of a new relationship between Nayan, Amber, Nina and Rowena. They gave themselves permission to get closer, more intimate. Nayan would often bring Rowena over to take Amber and Nina for a picnic. Their picnic on the grounds of the *Qutub Minar*, was a wonderful afternoon of the four of them getting to know each other. They also got a history lesson from Nayan. He was a fund of information.

"Look at this tall minaret in its red sandstone glory. It stands testament to one of the biggest power shifts in Delhi's history. In the 12th century, Mohammad Ghori ousted the Rajputs, and his successor, Qutub-ud-din Aibak laid the foundation for the Delhi Sultanate. This skyscraping 238-feet minaret was built to commemorate this victory," Nayan told them.

"May we climb the minaret, Papa?' Rowena asked.

"After we have finished eating, I'll take you all up."

They ate their sandwiches leisurely. There were no leftovers so they dusted the sheet they sat on and walked to the minaret.

In the main courtyard facing *Quwat-ul-Islam* Mosque that stood beside the *minar*, was a tall pillar.

"This is the Iron Pillar!" Nina exclaimed. A tourist stood with her back firmly against the pillar, and tried to make the fingers of both hands touch while holding the pillar in a backwards embrace. There was laughter and teasing from her family.

"I heard that if you can touch the fingers of both your hands, you can make a wish that will come true," Nina said.

"Very few succeed. There is nothing in history about this, but this story has stuck though the years. It probably got started by a tour guide," Nayan replied smiling. "This pillar dates back to 4th century A.D, to honor the Hindu god, Vishnu. It is made of iron, but in 1,600 years it hasn't decomposed or rusted. It is a great example of excellence in metallurgy."

"Nina, let's both of us circle our hands together around the pillar. Then we'll be able to span it. All our wishes will come true! But never mind. My wish has already come true," Rowena exclaimed.

"And which wish was that?" Nayan asked

laughing.

"That Miss Amber would be my mother and Nina would be my sister," Rowena replied.

Amber gave Rowena a hug. "I love you, my sweet one," she said gently and Nayan and Nina smiled.

"Papa, what language is this?" Rowena asked at the entrance as she looked at the outer walls of the structure.

"Arabic. Some of these are verses from the Quran, while others tell of the tower's history, and describe the changes and renovations made through the ages."

Each of the five floors had a balcony facing out to the gardens. Nayan and Rowena made a game of the climb, by counting the steps. By the time they reached the 378th step, they were all out of breath.

When they looked out, they could see all of Delhi. Nayan pointed the different landmarks from the Qutub. "There is *Hauz Khaz* on the left. It's the water tank built by Allauddin Khilji to supply water to his city. Over there you can see the walls of Tughlaqabad built by Ghazi Malik, the leader of the Tughlak dynasty. Over there is *Jama Masjid,* a mosque built by Shah Jahan, but it is also the area where you can taste some of the best Muslim cooking."

***

After two lonely years without Murad, Amber felt lighthearted and happy again. She loved Nayan and Rowena. Her love for Nayan was not so much a sharp, urgent need, as a long, slow pulse of dawning awakening to the reality that Murad was not coming back to her, and that he was not the only male she could be responsive to.

156

The next three weeks were Amber's happiest in two years. When Nayan was in town, he would take Amber out, or they made a foursome with Nina and Rowena. When Aparna or any other cousins were at the Vij home, Nayan generously invited all of them. Amber's family and extended family took to Nayan. Mrs. Kapoor and Mrs. Vij developed a close friendship.

Nayan was considerate and caring. He talked to her about her needs, hopes, and aspirations, and he listened attentively to her answers. This is what she had missed since she had lost Murad, she acknowledged. She had needed someone to share her ups and downs, no matter how trivial. Her in-laws, although kind-hearted and loving, had not probed into how she felt, or what her thoughts were on her life. Maybe, she too had blocked emotions and feelings from her life. But not anymore.

***

Okara, Pakistan January 1950
Murad woke up with a jerk. His breathing was ragged. He'd had the same dream every night for over two years. He raked his hair with a shaky hand.

If only he could remember. He recalled riding in a truck when the driver hit a huge rock. Murad's door had flown open and he had been thrown out about fifty feet. He had rushed back to save the driver but found the driver was dead. Flames were beginning to rise in the truck. He had to run fast to be safe. In his hurry, he had tripped, hitting his head on a sharp rock. Everything went black.

A farmer, Ayub Jaffrey, had run out to help him when he heard the explosion and carried him into his house. Murad was unconscious for a day, so the farmer

157

took him to a local hospital. He was treated for his cuts and bruises but the hospital personnel couldn't do anything about his memory. His life had begun two and a half years ago when he woke up on a bed in Ayub Jaffrey's house facing a metaphorical blank wall. His past may forever be hidden from him.

To have no past was a frightening thing. Even now Murad felt it difficult to accept. Ayub had behaved like a father. He nursed him back to health and gave him a room in his house till he knew where he wanted to go.

Ayub Jaffrey had told Murad that he knew his name was Murad Mehra because a week after the accident, some C.I.D officers had arrived at his house with a photo of Murad with his name. They had asked him if he had seen the man in the picture.

"I told them I'd never seen your face before. I don't know why those Criminal Investigation Department officers were looking for you. My intuition told me that *you* could be trusted. I wasn't so sure about them. During the partition a lot of finger pointing took place in both India and Pakistan. Usually people in high positions or the very rich were the target. They were imprisoned on some trumped-up charge, and heavy bribes were required for their release," explained Ayub, "I knew you were in no condition to undergo interrogation. You are still not well, so I suggest you lie low. If you like, you can help me with my farm in the meantime."

Murad had done just that. It seemed he was good with numbers and could help Ayub save money by economizing in some areas and buying new equipment for other tasks. Ayub told him he needed a

158

loan for new equipment, which the banks had refused. Murad suggested collective farming, not like the collective farms in Europe, but a form where neighboring farmers shared the equipment and the cost of the equipment. Murad wrote out a plan to show the rest of the farmers. The poor farmers agreed to his idea. It would mean more productivity with fewer costs.

Murad took his plan to a local bank to get a loan. The chief loan officer was so impressed by his articulate and knowledgably made plan, he'd told Murad that he would like to offer him a job to work under him. The officer would teach him everything he knew.

"I know you are a man who will go far. I'll look forward to working with you."

Murad agreed because he needed to be independent. He still helped Ayub and the farmers with their accounts with his innate business sense, but he was happy to work at the bank. He felt at home there. His boss demanded a lot from him but he also admired the speed with which Murad picked up on bank details.

The doctor treating him for his amnesia had long since given up hope of eliciting any change in his condition. In many ways it was almost a relief. Going over the same arid ground was a pointless exercise. If he ever recovered his memory, it would be if someone, or something, rewired a burned-out fuse. These were troubled times. At least with Ayub, he was safe with his new identity.

Murad's dream

A woman called out to him in his dream. She was the same woman who beckoned him in every dream. It was a dream devoid of color. This woman came like a black and white sketch. Except for her eyes. The color of her eyes was amber. He recognized this color was significant in his life. Amber. He tried to call out to her to take him with her but his voice remained mute. He tried to reach out to her, to touch her. She slipped away. But in this dream, the woman did not call out to him. She touched him, as if to say 'goodbye' and faded away in his dream. He felt that something very precious had left him. He didn't want that.

Murad awoke with an accelerated heartbeat. His head throbbed. He massaged his forehead with unsteady hands. He let out a sharp breath, his hazel eyes swept over the familiar room. He was on a cot in Ayub Jaffrey's house. He was sure the woman that came in his dream meant something in his life. Who was she? Why was she triggering that dream? Jerking upright, he searched for a trigger that may have caused this recurring dream, but his current memory, usually sharp and accurate, failed him.

Two years should have accustomed him to the blank space in his head after the accident. Although he'd given up on futile attempts to remember, his lost history frustrated him. Sometimes he felt like a prisoner in a dark room.

The bedside clock informed him that sunrise was too near to try for more sleep. He needed space and fresh air. Outside on the veranda he inhaled deeply, relishing the crisp morning air. His heart rate slowed down. He would be okay. His life would revert to normal.

He would find his amber, a stone or a woman, he would find out. He would remember. With each dream the woman had become more forceful. It was like she was willing herself into his consciousness. But today the force was gone. He wanted to hold on to the dream because he suspected he wouldn't have this dream again.

"You woke up early today, Murad *bhai*," said Noor, Ayub Jaffrey's 27-year-old daughter. "I hope you did not have another of your bad dreams. Would you like a cup of ginger tea with honey? It might make your headache go away."

"Thank you, *shukriya* Noor. "I do have a headache, and tea sounds good."

Noor was a young widow with an eight-year-old son, Rahim. When her husband died during a riot, his family ostracized Noor and her son, and one day they asked her to leave the house. A widow was unlucky to have in their midst.

Furtively, she'd packed their meager belongings, her jewelry, and all her savings. She was afraid a family member might see her packing and decide to take the savings and jewelry away.

With her money, she bought a train ticket to Okara to see her father. Her father was a very loving man and took to Rahim immediately. Noor's mother had died of jaundice four years earlier, so Noor took up the responsibility of housekeeping and cooking.

Rahim joined a local school. There was instant love between grandfather and grandson. Ayub taught him about nature and how seasons effect the crops. He talked about the constellations in the sky. Ayub taught him everything he knew about farming and Rahim loved to spend time outdoors and helped to tend to the crops. However, both Rahim's mother and his

161

grandfather made sure he went to school and knew the importance of an education.

Rahim took a shine to Murad who always talked to him like an equal. He did not talk down to him the way some adults had in his father's house. His 'Uncle Murad' looked so distinguished, Rahim wanted to be just like him.

Murad also loved the vulnerable little boy. He guided him with his homework. *How did he remember how to do mathematics?* Murad wondered. *How did he have such an acute business sense? He could read and write. He spoke Urdu, Hindi, and English fluently. Then how had the memory blocked out his personal life? His emotional life?*

Noor brought back a tray with tea and two cups. She also brought out a plate of homemade *khattais*, cookies.

"I thought I would join you before I get busy with my daily routine." She smiled sweetly at Murad who drank deeply. He emptied his cup and leaned forward to pour himself another cup.

"Let me," Noor said gently. "You work too hard and you haven't fully recovered."

"Surely I'm not so sick that I can't pour tea in a cup?"

"I'm worried about you Murad, *bhai*. You have so many headaches. You don't sleep well. Maybe the work is too stressful for you. You are not well. Stay at home for a few days to rest. She placed her hand over his. I will take care of you."

Murad looked directly at Noor. "You have done so much for me already. You helped me to come back to life. I can't thank you enough."

"No, no she squeezed his hand. You have helped *Baba* so much. He loves you and always sings your praise."

Murad smiled. Ayub Jaffrey was a good man. He was a simple man but he never failed to give credit where it was due.

"Murad *beta*, our productivity has doubled and our operating costs have gone down, all because of your suggestions. News of our methods has spread around the country. A team of foreign scholars wants to visit our farm next Monday. Will you stay at home that day? I won't understand their language, but you speak English, and after all, it was your plan. You know how to explain what we are doing."

Sure, *Baba*. I'll be glad to. I must go to work now, but I wanted to tell you that I have started to look for a flat near the bank. I have accepted your hospitality for too long. I can never thank you enough for all you have done for me, and I want you to know that if you ever need me, you just have to ask.

"Stay," Ayub Jaffrey implored. "Be my *damaad*, my son-in-law, and this house will be yours. You will also inherit my farm."

"*Baba*, I love Rahim like he were my son. Noor is a beautiful woman, inside and out. I am grateful for all she has done for me. But *Baba*, I can't take that step until I know about my past.

***

During a break at work, Murad checked with colleagues to see if they had heard of any vacant flats, for rent, in the area. He had stayed too long at Ayub Jaffrey's house. He could see that Noor was becoming more than fond of him and he had ignored that. She was a child

163

after all.

He must be in his forties, and she was only twenty-seven. He was nearly twenty years her senior. She was mature for her years, and she cared for him selflessly. But right now marriage, for him, seemed impossible. He couldn't drag another person into his darkness.

Javed, a co-worker, recommended a flat right next to the one his sister and brother-in-law lived in. A visiting professor lived there now, but he planned to return to his country at the end of the month. Javed would arrange for Murad and the professor to meet that afternoon. The two might come to an agreement.

The professor was a tall American with penetrating blue eyes and a firm handshake. He wore jeans, a blue sweater and Pakistani leather slippers. He was glad to show Murad around his flat. His furniture was beautiful. It had been ordered from a local dealer.

"I'd like to sell the furniture before I leave. I haven't had time to advertise it, but if you would like to buy it, that would help," the professor told him.

They discussed a price for all the furniture in the house, and Murad agreed to buy it.

"Will your landlord rent this flat to me?" Murad asked.

"I'll ask him today. I'm sure he will agree, especially as he won't have to sell the furniture before he rents this place out again."

Murad didn't say anything. He felt sure that the furniture could sell for much more than what the professor was asking for it.

"I'll let you know within a week," the professor concluded.

164

Murad reached the farm feeling like a weight had lifted from over his head.

Rahim ran to him to give him a big hug. Ayub followed his grandson, smiling.

"This boy has missed you. He wants you to help him with his mathematics homework."

"I'll be glad to do that. Would you like to sit at the dining table?"

"Yes, that will give us room, and dinner won't be ready for a few hours," Rahim agreed.

"Rahim!" admonished his mother. "Uncle Murad has just returned from work. You must give him some time to relax. Let him at least enjoy a cup of tea before you get started." She brought with her a tea tray with biscuits and a slice of cake.

"Thank you, Noor," Murad said, smiling up at her. "I can really use a hot cup of tea right now. But we can work at the same time. Come on, Rahim. Take out your math book."

Noor poured the tea as the two males worked together. She sat at the table affectionately watching them both.

***

Murad had been such a help to Rahim. Even Noor's husband had not taken such an interest in his own son. He had allowed Noor to take over the business of child raising. But Murad talked to Rahim as an equal. If Rahim had a question, Murad replied thoughtfully as if what Rahim asked was important.

She had never met a man like him. He was sincere, hardworking, affectionate, and so very good-looking. She couldn't help falling in love with him. But Murad wouldn't be interested in a woman like her. She wasn't educated beyond Middle School, while he had the air of a well-educated person. He seemed to come from a good background. He could never be interested in a farmer's daughter. And yet, he seemed to love and respect her father. Her father clearly loved and admired Murad.

"You haven't forgotten about tomorrow, have you Murad? The foreign team arrives here to check on our methods." Ayub Jaffrey questioned.

"No *Baba*, I did not. I asked my boss for a day off," Murad replied.

***

Tuesday, Okara, Pakistan 1950
The team arrived early in the morning in a large van. Murad, Mr. Jaffrey and the farmers were waiting. While the others disembarked, the first person out walked up to the group with a huge smile and shook their hands.

"I'm Roger Cook. I'm with the Fulbright group. We heard about your methods of farming and were impressed. We would love to see how your methods work."

Murad translated. The farmers nodded and smiled.

"They say it is a pleasure to have you visit," Murad replied.

Soon the rest of the group joined them. One member, Eric Jeffers, kept glancing at him as if expecting Murad to say something. The man's face was familiar. It was as if Murad had seen him somewhere, maybe in another lifetime.

After Murad had conducted the tour over the farms and explained how the farms interacted, the team returned to Ayub Jaffrey's home to have lunch. All the farmers' wives were there. They had helped Noor in the kitchen to prepare the lunch.

The team was impressed with the farming efforts and enjoyed the lunch very much.

Eric turned to Murad. "You don't recognize me, do you?"

Murad shook his head. "Your face is familiar. It is as if I have seen you before. Unfortunately, I had a head injury two and half years ago and can't remember my life before that. Do you know me?"

Eric combed his fingers through his hair. "**Two and half years?** Yes, I know you. I'm Ambika's husband. She was your wife, Amber's, best friend."

AMBER?!!. Murad felt suddenly dizzy and his head started to pound. He put his hands to his head.

"Hey, I didn't mean to upset you," Eric exclaimed. "But there are people looking for you. I know what your parents, your wife and children went through. They were frantic. They called the border patrol. Your friend at the C.I.D sent his men looking for you."

"C.I.D.? My friend? Ayub thought they had come to arrest me! So he didn't tell them about me. I was in the hospital at the time. He felt I would not be able to withstand the interrogation."

Eric laughed shakily. "A good friend, though a little misguided. Will you come back home with me to meet Ambika and our two adopted children? Then we can figure out what to do next?"

Murad nodded. "I hate to leave Ayub suddenly like this. But I was planning on moving out at the end of the month."

Lahore

Murad explained to Ayub, Rahim, and Noor what he must do. He would leave with Eric Jeffers to find out about his past.

"When I find out where I am going to be, I will write to you so you can contact me if you ever need me," Murad told them.

They hugged and cried. Murad called his work to let them know he needed a month's leave of absence. His boss had grown close to him and told him he understood. Murad needed his life back.

He rode back with the team to Lahore. In the van, Eric told Murad a little bit about his life, fearing he might cause a setback. But Murad was ready to hear. He had been ready for two years.

"You have a wife, Amber, and two children, Neil and Nina. Neil is studying at Oxford, England, and your daughter, Nina lives with your parents and your wife in Shimla, in India. Amber writes to Ambika, so I know she is the vice-principal of a school that Nina attends."

Murad listened. None of this seemed to bring him to familiar ground.

"Do you remember your dear friend, Howard Skinner?"

"No," Murad replied hesitantly shaking his head.

"He insisted on taking Neil with him to England to see if he could get him a scholarship at a college there. Neil received a scholarship at Oxford with Howard's help. He is Neil's guardian in England. Neil sees him during his vacations."

Murad nodded. If only he could remember. There were odd flashes from time to time, but nothing concrete.

"Tell me when to stop, Murad. I don't want your brain to go on overload. I don't want to feed you *my* ideas about your life in Lahore. But you spent most of your married life in that city. With luck there will be some recognition when you see it again. Ambika will be waiting at home to give you extra support. I called her earlier and explained the situation. She is so excited. She has missed you and Amber. "

"Don't worry, Eric. My brain was already on overload when we left Okara. I have so many questions. What kind of job did I have when you knew me?"

Eric smiled. "You were a banker. You were the president of National Grindlays Bank."

"No wonder, I knew so much about banking. It came naturally to me!" Murad exclaimed.

"Amber was a school teacher?"

"No Amber was a respected jewelry designer. People came to her for her unusual designs. My wife, Ambika, has a lot of jewelry designed by Amber. Both our wives are artists. Your wife, Amber, created jewelry, and my Ambika loves to paint. But Amber also had a teaching degree, which she decided to use when it seemed necessary.

Murad nodded. "I have heard of Ambika's art. She is a well-known artist. I have seen some of her paintings of village scenes and her depiction of the local countryside."

"We have many photographs of the four of you. Ambika used one photograph to paint your family portrait. It is beautiful, but she has never exhibited it.

The painting is too personal for her."

"Maybe the photographs will help jog my memory. Thank you, Eric, for offering me this chance to become whole again. I can't afford to turn my back on your offer. This might be my only chance to remember."

When the van driver dropped off Murad and Eric at the house, his wife Ambika was waiting anxiously on the front veranda. She ran out to meet them. She hugged her husband and then hugged Murad.

"Oh, Murad! It is so good to see you alive and well. Let me look at you."

Her artist's eyes scanned his face. "You have changed so much. But come in, come in. I've been waiting for you ever since Eric informed me he had met you. We have missed you so much. Amber will be so happy to know you are well."

Murad recognized Ambika from the photographs he had seen of her in newspapers. She was a world-renowned artist, after all. But he didn't have any personal memories of their friendship.

Ambika guided the two men to the living room. Eric excused himself to freshen up. Ambika leaned forward towards Murad. "Tell me what you have been doing for the past two years."

Murad tried to give her a short version of what he had undergone. He had tried to remember, but it seemed he had left his past behind forever.

"Don't say that," Ambika *hushed* him. "Let me show you some photographs of all of us together. Maybe it will jog your memory." She went to bring out some photo albums.

Murad flipped through the albums with her but

none of the tiny two-by-three photos jogged his memory.

"Wait," Ambika said. "Let me bring you the painting I made of the four of you." She returned with a large canvas. The painting was exquisite. Murad's face was turned towards Amber with a tender, loving expression. Amber had her arms around her two children who leaned against her.

In the painting it seemed that the whole family leaned on Amber for support. And suddenly it all came back to him. His first meeting with Amber and their life together. How could he have forgotten such a beautiful part of his life? How could he have let his whole family down?

Murad closed his eyes hoping the sudden pounding in his head would stop. But the pain only intensified and his head began to throb. Murad held his head as it seemed to explode with the pain. He shook his head in despair. "How could fate have played such a cruel trick on me that I abandoned my family? I let them all down when they most needed me." There was a raw pain in Murad's voice.

Ambika held his hands. "You are lucky, Murad. You are still alive. You are healthy. Your family is safe. You have been blessed with a second chance. Take it and make a new life for yourself with Amber and your children. Your parents are waiting anxiously as well."

They were interrupted by running feet and giggles of two children. Eric and Ambika's children returned from school with their nanny. They threw their books near the front door and ran to hug their parents. "*Ammi*, Papa!"

Ambika and Eric had adopted these two

171

beautiful, fair, rosy-cheeked, healthy siblings-Asiah, seven, and Sadik nine. They had been left orphaned during the partition.

"Asiah and Sadik, this is your Uncle Murad. He has a daughter and a son as well. You will enjoy meeting them."

The children hugged Murad. "We're hungry, *Ammi*. Is lunch ready?"

"Of course," Ambika told them fondly. "Go wash up. We will all eat together."

"How are you feeling now, Murad? Would you like an asprin?"

"No, I think I will be okay. It will be easier for me to move forward, now that I remember. I feel like I have my life back."

Over lunch, Eric and Ambika tried to figure out a strategy to get Murad back into India.

"Crossing over the Lahore border to Wagah might be too dangerous. There are four checkpoints. Anyone crossing the border is regarded with suspicion," Ambika said.

"That's true," agreed Eric. "Let me talk to Murad's old friend, Yusuf, at the C.I.D. office to see if he has any suggestions. I'll go alone."

The next morning Eric went to see Yusuf while Ambika drove Murad around Lahore to show him the city he had left behind. Lahore was so green. In spite of the chill in the air, the parks were crowded. Children played cricket, families picnicked, vendors roasted corncobs for sale, and grandparents walked peacefully. The effect of the partition was not apparent.

"Lahore is so beautiful," Murad remarked, and Ambika nodded.

"It is a special city. There are five specific seasons. It has history, culture, and some of the most famous artists can call Lahore their home.

"Shehr e Lahore teri ronaqien dayem aabaad
Teri galiyon ki hawa kheinch ke layee mujh ko,"
Murad quoted the poet, Nasir Kazmi.

Ambika smiled and translated the verse: *"My city Lahore. May your warmth and passion last forever. It is the air of your streets that pulls me back to you.* What made you remember that couplet?"

Murad looked puzzled and with tears in his eyes said, "I don't know." Then he smiled at Ambika, "I will miss this city and my life here. But I can't wait to get back to my family."

***

"Murad is alive?" Yusuf Sayani exclaimed. "But we looked all over for him. My men searched every nook and cranny of areas where he might have been." He raised his hands in the air. "Thanks Allah, my friend is alive. I'll come home with you, Eric, to meet him. Then we can decide how to get him to India. I can't wait to see my good friend, Murad."

***

"Let me look at you, Murad *bhai*, my brother, my friend!" Yusuf Sayani said cupping his friend's face and kissing his forehead. "It is so good to see you alive and healthy." He shook his head. "Do you know how long we searched for you? Your beloved wife refused to believe me when I told her we had seen the incinerated truck you were on. She would book a call every day to check if we had any news."

Yusuf looked embarrassed. "I am sorry, *bhai*. Even *I* thought you had died along with so many others

173

who had lost their lives during this partition between our two countries. Maybe this was Allah's way of keeping you safe. He works in mysterious ways."

Yusuf hugged Murad again. "But now we must find a way to get you back to your family."

"Thank you, Yusuf *bhai*," Murad said, smiling now. "I will always be in your debt if you can help me."

"Let's sit outside in the garden. The weather is so pleasant." Ambika guided them to chairs outside. She asked the housekeeper to bring out the tea along with *samosas* and cookies.

Eric, Murad, and Ambika sat around Yusuf Sayani, waiting to hear what he had in mind.

"Murad, do you still have your Indian passport?" Yusuf asked.

"I do, actually. It was in my wallet when Ayub Jaffrey found me. He kept my wallet safely for me, but then forgot about it. He returned it to me last month when he found it again in his desk drawer."

"Good. I'm attending a United Nations meeting in Geneva, to discuss how Pakistan and India can maintain peaceful relations in Kashmir. You are coming with me. There are several delegates attending from India as well. One of the delegates from India is Ritesh Khanna. Do you remember him?"

"Yes, of course I do. I didn't know he was involved in politics now. He used to work at my bank."

"Ritesh has reached out to me for citizens needing to return to Pakistan safely. I have helped him. Now it will be my turn to ask him a favor."

"What kind of favor, Yusuf?" Eric asked.

"Murad will fly out of Pakistan with me, but he will return to India with Ritesh. I will talk to him when

I meet him in Geneva," Yusuf replied, grinning.

"I don't want us to do anything illegal, Yusuf *bhai*. I don't want you getting into trouble," Murad protested.

"We will do nothing illegal. We will just cut through the bureaucracy. Now let's go about getting you some clothes, Murad. I know a tailor who is fast and very good. Let's go to him now."

***

Murad stood in front of the *Palais des Nations* situated in a beautiful park overlooking Lake Geneva with a splendid view of the Alps and the famous Mont Blanc. There were flags of all the countries that had signed the charter to abide by the decisions of the United Nations. He saw the Indian tricolored flag waving in the wind. He felt a sense of pride, awe, and wonder to be able to stand in front of this stately building which had once housed the *League of Nations*.

His thoughts went back to his conversation with Eric and Ambika on that last night in Lahore before he flew to Geneva. He had shared with them how he had dreamed of Amber every night. It had seemed as if she was calling out to him. When he told them he had felt that Amber was saying 'goodbye' the last time he had dreamed of her, he had watched Eric and Ambika look at each other.

Eric had cleared his throat. "Murad, there is something you have to know before you return to India."

"What do you want to tell me?" Murad had asked.

"Well, uh um, I don't know how to say it any differently but there is another man in Amber's life."

175

"Amber's remarried, and you didn't think to tell me earlier?" Murad was stunned.

"No, no!" Ambika exclaimed. "Amber would never do that without the approval of her parents and children. She will wait until Neil comes home in July. Your parents and her parents have encouraged this match. They felt it would not be easy for Amber to live without a husband by her side to protect her. People look down on single women trying to make it on their own. Your parents felt they were not going to be around forever to watch over Amber and your children."

"What kind of a man am I that I let my family down when they most needed me?" Murad exclaimed.

"It's nobody's fault, Murad," Ambika placated. "Fate dealt you a hand. You did what you could with it. So did Amber."

He hadn't seen Amber for more than two years. Had she changed? Would she want him back the way he was? He had changed. He had learned how hard it was to toil in the fields. He had worked alongside Ayub. He was no longer just a banker. The title of President was just that. It could be given or taken away at a whim. Life offered no security. It just offered challenges. Murad hadn't allowed the challenges to stop him; he had used them to become stronger and to grow. He had learned so much from his friend, Ayub. Sometimes, in a low moment, he had considered his life as a glass half full but it was ready to be filled to the brim now. Amber and his children were his life. He would fight for them. For the first time in over two years, his future suddenly seemed full of promise.

***

The delegates filed in to take their seats at the United

176

Nations Office at Geneva (UNOG). Murad sat in the back row with some audience members. The meeting came to order. There were several items to be discussed, but finally it was time for the Kashmir question. The head of the United Nations Commission on India and Pakistan stood up.

"We are here to resolve the crisis in Jammu and Kashmir. At the end of the colonial rule of the United Kingdom, both the Commission and the Security Council decided that the future of Jammu and Kashmir would be decided by the plebiscite of the people in that area. In 1949, the Security Council established a "line of control" (the LOC) between the part seized by India in 1948 and the part of Kashmir under Pakistani influence (Azad Kashmir).

"We have received and noted the report of General A.G.L. McNaughton. We would like to commend the Governments of India and Pakistan for their statesman like action in reaching the agreements embodied in the United Nations Commission's resolutions of August 13, 1948 and January 5, 1949 for cease-fire, for the demilitarization of the State of Jammu and Kashmir..."

Murad admired the work of the United Nations in maintaining peace around the world. From his peripheral vision, he could see Ritesh Khanna sitting along with the Indian delegates. Would Ritesh be able to help him? Murad and Amber had become close to his family during Ritesh's sister's wedding. But that was several years ago.

As the delegates walked towards the exit doors, Yusuf approached Ritesh.

"Ritesh *bhai*, how are you doing?"

177

"*Well,* thank you, with God's mercy," Ritesh replied. "Thank you for all your help in taking the migrants to safety."

Yusuf shook his head. "That was my duty."

Just then Murad walked up behind Yusuf.

"S-s sir! Murad sir!" Ritesh stuttered. "I-I thought... I heard." He never completed his sentence. "I never thought I would get a chance to thank you, in person, sir. You warned me to leave Lahore with my family before a partition took place. I took your advice. For that reason alone my family is safe today. You even recommended me for a position at the bank in New Delhi."

Murad smiled. "Look at you now! You are a Congressite in Nehru's team, a politician."

Ritesh smiled back.

"It is the least I can do for my country."

"Ritesh, we need your help. Will you do something for us?" Yusuf asked.

Ritesh looked confused. "How can I help?"

"May we talk privately, in your room, perhaps?"

"Of course."

In his room, Murad and Yusuf explained to Ritesh what they needed for him to do. Ritesh's eyes shone with unshed tears. He was overwhelmed.

"Murad sir, you have done so much for me and my family. You took care of all the wedding functions at my sister's wedding when her in-laws started to make demands of a dowry. My father would not have been able to afford the wedding if it hadn't been for you and your beautiful wife. Both of you took on the responsibility. You helped me reestablish myself in a new town and a new country. How can you ask me *if* I will do as you ask? I only ask your permission to share this information with my rooming colleague. He is also the lead delegate. I will explain everything to him. Just be at the airport by 11 a.m. tomorrow."

That evening, Murad booked a call to Shimla and another to Howard Skinner in London. The phone call to India was received through a lot of static.

"Hello! Hello!" someone shouted on the other end.

"Are Vij sahib or memsahib there?" Murad asked loudly.

"Hello! Hello! This is Raghu, housekeeper. I can't hear you. Oh no! My vegetables are burning. I have to go." The phone disconnected with a click. Murad and Yusuf shook their heads.

The call to Howard was clear. Murad explained to a very pleased and surprised Howard that he was still alive. He thanked him for helping Neil and his family. Howard promised to tell Neil the good news that his father was alive.

The next morning, Yusuf and Murad parted company promising to keep in touch. Ritesh was waiting with the lead man, Suresh Thakur.

"Murad sir, please give your passport to Mr. Thakur. He is collecting all the passports for his team of delegates and taking them into customs."

The procedures went smoothly. Suresh Thakur guided Murad to sit with him in the front. No one commented on the new person joining the group. He was with their leader, after all. Maybe he was someone from the team who had flown in earlier. Maybe he was an important official. No one asked.

Shimla, March 1950

Nayan knocked softly at Amber's office door and walked in. Luckily, Amber was alone. He lifted her from her chair.

"Come on. Let's go," he said twirling her around away from her desk. "We're celebrating."

"Celebrating what?" demanded Amber, laughing.

"Celebrating life, "Nayan responded, grinning. "Life, love, you, the spring equinox."

"How was your meeting in Bombay?" Amber gasped.

"It went well, but I missed you." He lowered his head to kiss her cheek. Then raising her chin, he lowered his lips to her own.

"Nayan! Anyone can walk in. What if Mother Superior came?"

"Let's get out of here. I'll bring you back in an hour."

Amber explained to the office clerk in the next room that she was stepping out for lunch and would be back soon.

The clerk smiled at her affectionately. He was an old man and had become very fond of Amber during her time at the school.

Amber joined Nayan as he hustled her towards his car. She laughed giddily. She was so happy to see Nayan again. "Where are we going?"

Nayan smiled at her. "You have such a lovely, uncomplicated, natural laugh. Has anyone ever told you that?"

Amber stilled. Murad had always loved her

laugh. How did she suddenly think of him? She thought she had finally made her peace with his memory. So why did she feel guilty for feeling happy with Nayan?

***

Shimla, April 1950

It was Friday evening. The days were getting warmer. After dropping Rowena at her friend, Sonia's, to spend the night, Nayan drove Amber and Nina to the local club to play tennis. Nina was scheduled to play a game with her friend, and Nayan had persuaded Amber to play with him.

"I haven't played tennis in years. I'm sure I'm not in your league," Amber had protested.

"Don't worry. I'll watch your game and match it," Nayan reassured.

Nayan won the first and second set but Amber got better and won the third set.

"Did you let me win on purpose?" she accused breathlessly.

"I would never do that," Nayan said shaking his head. "I hate to lose. You are quick and agile. Your focus and speed were impressive. You're a formidable opponent."

Amber laughed. "Now I know you are teasing me. But I'm going to stop when I'm on top of my game!" Nayan couldn't help responding with the same carefree laughter.

He enjoyed spending time with Amber. He was happy his wait would be over in three months when Neil came home and he and Amber could get married. He knew Nina approved of him. He would make sure Neil liked him too because he had learned that Amber and her children were a package deal.

"Let's find Nina. I think she and her friend are using that court on the right," Amber said pointing to where the two girls were playing.

"If she wants to play for a little longer, we can go in for a cup of tea," Nayan suggested, but Nina was ready. They had just finished their game.

He drove the two women home. He parked his car under the covered porch and walked them into the living room. There was a man standing in the middle of the living room flanked by Murad's parents who were talking to him animatedly.

"Amber, Nina! Look who's back?" Mrs. Mehra exclaimed.

"Murad is alive! This is the best surprise we could get!" said Murad's father, grinning broadly.

"Papa!" Nina flew into her father's arms. Murad kissed the top his daughter's head while he clutched her in a tight embrace and then looked directly into Amber's eyes.

898

The floor rocked under Amber's feet, but her collapsing muscles were supported up by Nayan. There was a dreamlike unreality to that moment. It was almost a nightmare. It was a cruel joke for someone to stand in the living room and masquerade as Murad and mimic his voice.

She stared at the tall figure in front of her. The man had Murad's wide forehead, strong chin, and bridged nose. But this man did not have his fair skin. It was dark and weathered, giving a harshness to his face.

This man's eyes were the familiar hazel color,

but they now wore a narrow hooded look, as they seemed to pierce into her soul. His hair was the same dark brown, but its waving thickness was longer than Murad had worn it, giving the impression of being unruly instead of smoothly in place. Murad never had his hair out of place. He had looked like a banker with short hair, perfectly fitted suits and polished shoes. This man was as tall as Murad but his build was more muscular.

The differences registered with the speed of lightning, while the rest of her reeled from the similarities. The buzzing in her head continued nonstop, facts clicking into place.

Murad was alive. He was standing in this room. She should go to him. Nayan had released his hold on her. She swayed forward. "You're alive!" And then merciful blackness overwhelmed her as she slid to the floor in a faint.

Murad intercepted Nayan from carrying Amber to her bed. Amber opened her eyes to find Murad sitting up next to her on the bed. He looked worried. "That's better." He stroked her hair away from her forehead. "I'm sorry that my arrival was such a shock."

Amber pushed him away from her. "What took you so long to come back?" she accused him bitterly.

"I had an accident and lost my memory. Can you ever forgive me for not being there for you when you needed me?"

"When did you start to remember again?" Amber asked. She was surprised to see the vulnerability on Murad's face.

"Two weeks ago."

"Two weeks, and you didn't think you should

call?" Amber asked.

"I did. The housekeeper answered the phone. He said no one was home and he had to run as his vegetables were burning!" Murad grinned.

Amber laughed weakly. "Did you try a second time?"

"You know how difficult it is to get a call through. After I recovered my memory, I wanted to be with you as soon as possible. Even traveling to India has been a sort of miracle in my life. The border authorities would have made it very difficult for me to get through," Murad explained.

"How did you get back?"

"That's a long story and I'll save it for another time," Murad replied.

"There is something I need to tell you."

"Is it about Nayan?"

Amber nodded.

"I know already. Ambika and Eric told me about him. You are a beautiful woman, Amber. How can any man not want to be with you?"

"You don't mind?" Amber asked.

"You didn't cheat on me, Amber. You thought I was dead. So did everybody else."

"I feel so guilty," Amber whispered.

"Actually, when I saw you walk in with Nayan, your face was turned towards him and you were laughing. I saw the way he looked at you. He is crazy about you. I thought for a fraction of a second how much better it might be for you to be loved by someone uncomplicated, with no dark past," Murad said.

"You want me to divorce you and marry Nayan?" Amber whispered.

"No, no, Amber! I said, for a fraction of a second, that altruistic thought entered my mind. It was dreams about you that kept me sane. It made me look forward to a life when I would remember. I would be a broken man without you. But I also want you to be happy. Do *you* want to be with me?" His gaze was like a warm summer morning and Amber basked in the heat.

"I'm glad you came back safely," Amber told him.

"Thank you for telling me that." He kissed her forehead. "Now we'd better go out to tell Nayan and the rest, you are okay."

"I'd like some time alone, please."

"Okay. I'll leave you by yourself, but I'll come back soon," Murad promised as he walked back into the living room.

"Amber is fine," he told his family and Nayan. "She just needs some time alone."

Nayan stood up. "Maybe I should go in to see how she is doing before I leave."

"Not right now, Nayan, I'm sorry. She needs some time to herself. I think my arrival gave her a bit of a shock. Maybe tomorrow. I'll see you out. I hope you don't mind but I think we all need some family time together." He put his arm around Nayan's shoulders, guiding him out.

"I know you and Amber were about to become engaged. That can't happen now that I'm back," Murad told Nayan firmly. "Amber is my wife, not my *widow,* and I don't want a divorce. I'm truly sorry for the way circumstances have unraveled, but you know there can be no continuation of your engagement now."

Nayan didn't bother to respond. He would talk

to Amber tomorrow and get her answer.

When Murad returned to the living room, his parents and Nina barraged him with questions. Where had he been? How did he return to India? Murad's story was like a fictional tale, but he told it the only way he could. The truth.

He and Amber had a lot to talk about. She had changed too. If anything, she was more beautiful than ever. The eyes he had seen in his dreams did not do the real ones justice. Her eyes were large and luminous amber, which turned to gold when she was angry. He had seen them change color when she'd asked him, furiously, why he had taken so long to return. Amber had always been beautiful, but she had done nothing to enhance her looks. Now she had learned to accentuate her eyes with light makeup. Her eyebrows were more arched, and the dark kohl emphasized her long, fine lashes. His heart had raced when he saw her walk into the room. He was unprepared for his reaction to her. Was he falling in love with his wife all over again? How had he lived without her for so long? He would do anything to keep her in his life.

Murad and Amber

That night Amber woke up to the sound of groans beside her. Murad was moving restlessly on his bed.

"Show me the way!" he muttered in his sleep. "Don't go!" he moaned, "please don't go!"

Amber walked over to his side. "Murad wake up! You are having a bad dream." Amber shook him awake. His eyes flew open. He looked at her with startled, unseeing eyes.

"Amber?" he whispered. "It was you I dreamed of. Don't ever leave me again." He reached out to bring her down close to him. "Please don't ever leave me, Amber," he muttered feverishly.

"I won't," Amber soothed.

"You promise?"

"I do. Now go back to sleep. I'm here by your side. Amber sat on a chair beside his bed, holding his hand."

Earlier Amber had thought of ways to tell Murad that she didn't know the new Murad, and she was confused about her feelings towards him. But now she realized she had always loved Murad and she would continue to love him no matter how he looked, how he spoke, or what experiences either of them had encountered. Her love was as steady and enduring as it had always been. Her feelings for Nayan had developed from the loneliness and the void she experienced when Murad did not return. She would talk to Nayan tomorrow.

Murad could see the early light of dawn when he woke up. Amber was sleeping on a chair near his bed. She had comforted him and stayed by his bedside when he had been awakened thinking he was lost.

Her wavy brown hair cascaded over her shoulders while a few tendrils had spilled over her face. He sat up and stroked her hair away from her face. "Good morning," he whispered. She opened her sleep filled eyes showing concern for Murad.

"Are you okay?" she asked.

Murad smiled. "I'm fine but you might find your body a little stiff from sleeping on this chair."

187

"You had a bad dream, last night."

"I know. It is a dream that has haunted me all the years I was away. I think you were trying to reach out to me. When I tried to follow, you disappeared," Murad explained.

He cupped her face. "I'm so glad that I have found you again. But please don't feel I will force you or pressure you to accept me back as your husband. I know you have made another life for yourself. You have become independent. I will leave the final decision up to you. All I ask is that you give our relationship another chance."

"When I found out you were missing or maybe even dead, I wanted to die along with you. But I knew your parents and Nina and Neil needed me. I had to be strong for them. For two years I mourned for you. I felt I should have been there for you. I wished I had sent Nina and Neil ahead of us to your parents. If I had been with you I might have been able to save you. Many nights I cried myself to sleep. When you came home, I wanted to run to you."

"You were in shock," Murad consoled.

"It wasn't just shock. It was also guilt because I had started dating Nayan. It was caution too. There you were, my husband. But you seemed so different, aloof, cold, wary, a stranger, someone I didn't know. The husband I knew was kind, sensitive, warm and sophisticated. The person standing in the room was distant, tanned, rough, and rugged."

Murad shook his head. "I suppose I've learned that the basics of life are more important. The rest is garnish. Fundamentally, I don't believe I have changed."

188

Amber smiled weakly. "I guess I got fooled and intimidated by the garnish."

"You should know me better than that."

"That's just it," Amber explained, "I didn't think I did because I saw the superficial changes in you."

"I guess I also expected everything to be the way it was, as if I hadn't been away for over two years. You have changed, too, Amber. You have an air of confidence about you, which you didn't have before and you are even more beautiful. But we'll both have to adjust to our growth as human beings. I'm willing to work on it, but I meant it when I said I want you to decide what you want. It will be painful if you decide to make your life with Nayan, but I will support your decision."

Amber shook her head. "I met Nayan just six months ago. His daughter, Rowena, attached herself to me, and I couldn't help loving the adorable little girl. She lost her mother when she was only two. She lived with her grandmother because Nayan was building his hotel business. One day Nayan came to my office to discuss Rowena's behavior in class."

"He must be a caring father."

"He is, Murad. He is sweet, loving, and kind. These were the qualities that attracted me, but Rowena was the glue in our relationship. We both loved her. I was hesitant to cement the relationship even after Nayan asked me to marry him, but your parents, and mine, encouraged me to move forward.

Murad nodded. "I understand, Amber. I also know that you have probably developed feelings for Nayan. I love you, but I can't demand that you feel the same way after two years. All I ask is that you think about what *you* want. You have taken care of others for too long."

"Okay," Amber smiled. "I should get ready for school." She stood up unsteadily. Her legs hurt and her body was stiff from sleeping on the chair. "Ow," she winced grabbing at her shoulder, "I did sleep in a very awkward position." Murad stood up also, the weight of his hands coming to rest on her shoulders. He swept Amber's hair over her shoulders and started to knead her muscles slowly and methodically.

Amber looked up into Murad's eyes. She saw his love and caring for her and her future. Her life stretched before her filled with endless possibilities. The two of them had shared so much and conquered darkness to reach this moment. They were bound together by their shared history and their love.

***

Murad insisted on walking with Amber and Nina to their school.

"I had forgotten how fresh and brisk the morning air is in Shimla. It is fun to walk," Murad said.

"Yes, but it is good that our school is not far from the house, or we would have to run every morning," Nina chuckled, clutching her father's arm. "Papa, I am so happy that Uncle Eric found you at the farm and took you home with him, or you might never have remembered us! You might still have been a *kisaan* laboring in someone's fields."

"I'm very grateful to Eric and Ambika for all they did for me. But don't look down on farming, Nina. If people like Ayub didn't work so hard, you wouldn't have food on the table. Farmers keep you alive."

190

"Well, I'm just glad you are alive and back with us. We were so worried. *Ammi* called friends and other officials in Pakistan every day to see if they had any news."

Murad glanced at Amber who was gazing up at him. Was that love he saw in her eyes? He hoped so. He couldn't let her go. His life would be meaningless unless she was there to share it with him. He placed his arms around Amber and Nina's shoulders hugging them close to him.

"I am truly sorry for all the pain and worry I have caused. Please, can you forgive me?"

"Oh, Papa, it wasn't your fault! You were injured. You lost your memory. I'm glad that you are back with us," Nina exclaimed turning to hug her father.

At the school gate, Amber left Nina to show Murad around the school as she went to join Mother Superior for morning assembly. Nina took her father to her classroom where she deposited her school bag.

"Come, Papa, we still have time. I will show you our school."

Nina was showing Murad the school grounds when they saw Nayan come in with Rowena. Rowena ran to give Nina a hug.

"Hi Nina *didi*. I had so much fun at Sonia's during the weekend, but I missed you. I like you best!"

Nina smiled affectionately at Rowena. She gave the younger girl a hug. "I love you too, little one."

Rowena looked at her mischievously. "You won't be able to call me 'little one' for long. I'm nearly as tall as you already."

Nina smiled at her. "Come, let me take you to

your class. Uncle Nayan, I will take her with me. Papa, It's time for our assembly. I will see you in the afternoon."

Nayan turned to Murad. "Would you like a ride home? Your house is on my way."

"Sure," Murad accepted. His body had not yet adjusted to the higher altitude. The uphill climb had tired him.

During the ride back, both the men were quiet for a while. "Your family must be happy to see you healthy and back with them," Nayan spoke eventually.

"They are. Thank you for being there for my family when I couldn't be."

"What happened to you?"

"I hit my head against a rock. As quickly as that happened, I lost my memory."

"I'm sorry. That must have been stressful for you."

Murad shrugged. "Life happens. My return must have been a shock for you. You love Amber. She is confused, too. Maybe she thinks she loves you. But Nayan, please know that her first loyalty will always be with me."

The car screeched to a halt in front of Murad's house. "I'm glad you have your memory back and are safe," said Nayan knowing that he could never wish ill health even on his worst enemy.

***

"Nayan, do you think we could meet for lunch today at noon?" Amber asked over the phone.

"Yes," Nayan answered, gratified that Amber had approached him. "I love you."

"I'll see you at lunch," Amber replied.

Amber was waiting for Nayan as he drove into the parking area. She walked up to his car. He bent down to kiss her forehead. "This is great. The lady I love is waiting for me." He guided Amber to the front seat of his car. "Where would you like to go?"

"Somewhere close," Amber replied.

"There is a restaurant right around the corner which opened last month. Would you like to try it out?"

"Sure."

When they were seated at their table Amber held out a jewelry box to give to Nayan.

"You mother gave it to me at our *roka*. I'll have the rest of the gifts returned, but I wanted to return the jewelry to you, personally."

"You are telling me, we are not getting married," Nayan said in a flat tone.

"I'm sorry," Amber replied.

"Look Amber, I know things aren't easy for you right now." He stopped and shook his head. "This isn't the time to burden you with my feelings. You know I love you, and will always be there for you."

Amber's eyes glistened with unshed tears. She reached out to touch his arm and then withdrew her hand. "I'm truly sorry, Nayan, but I've made up my mind. I'm not going to ask for a divorce. And I want you to move on as well. I was too old for you, anyway. You'll find a younger, more beautiful, more loving person to marry."

"It's not that easy," Nayan said angrily. "I have never loved a person like I have loved you, not even my wife. The marriage to my wife was arranged. I respected her, and probably even loved her, but not like I love you."

"You, Rowena, and your mother, will always have a special place in my heart. I'll talk to Rowena to explain, and she can always come to me or Nina if she wants to talk," Amber replied, "but I have a husband and my relationship with you cannot continue."

"If that's your decision, then I'll have to accept it," Nayan said grimly. "You haven't touched your food. Please eat."

"You haven't eaten either, Nayan. I guess we are both not very hungry," Amber replied sadly.

Nayan nodded. "Do you want me to take you back to school?"

"I think that would be best," Amber told him.

***

Deep down Nayan had known that Amber would choose her husband over him. Murad was the father of her children. They completed each other. So why did he feel so empty and sad? Against all odds, Amber had aroused within him the kind of protective, possessive, and intense love that he had not thought he was emotionally capable of experiencing. The rational side of his nature had warned him that he had fallen in love too quickly and too deeply, and that such emotions may not withstand the test of time. Right now, however, he couldn't think of a life without Amber, but he would move on. His daughter and mother needed him.

***

Amber's feelings of regret were so profound that it required a great effort not to let them engulf her. She walked home from school that afternoon with her mind in turmoil. She had hurt Nayan. She knew that he loved her deeply, and the curt firmness in her rejection had not played out as kindly as she had visualized. But how did one couch a rejection? She couldn't think of an alternative. She knew she had done the right thing. How could she even think of marrying Nayan?

"What's the matter, *Ammi*?" Nina asked as she walked beside her mother. "You look so sad."

Amber shook her head. "It's nothing. I was just thinking."

"You met Uncle Nayan, today. What happened?"

Amber looked at Nina in surprise. "How did you know I met him today?"

"I saw you getting out of his car during my afternoon recess," Nina explained. "Are you worried about how Uncle Nayan and Rowena will feel?"

"How did you guess?"

Nina spoke wryly. "Oh *Ammi*. I've known you for seventeen years. You are a softie. You try to be strong for all of us but your own heart melts when you see anyone hurt. But don't worry. It will all work out. Events take place in our lives for a reason. We don't always know why at the time.

"You could have fallen apart when you received the news about Papa. But you kept us all together. Neil went on to study in England. You explored a new career, and I was lucky to have a strong and loving *Ammi* by my side!" Nina gave her mother her a hug. "Papa learned to appreciate that all people are not bad. A Muslim farmer and many Muslim acquaintances in Pakistan took care of him. We all learned something from this. Now Papa is back. We are a family again."

"When did you become so wise?" Amber asked in wonder.

Nina smiled at her mother. "I don't know, but

195

you and Papa have been the perfect role models for both Neil and me.

Amber shook her head. "I don't feel strong. I just do what I think is practical and right at the moment."

"There is nothing wrong with being practical, *Ammi*. You took the practical route when our lives were falling apart. You built our family into something strong and enduring because you found a basis to build on. Uncle Nayan and Rowena came into our lives for a reason. They brought with them love, laughter, and hope. I think you and I enhanced their lives as well. They will be fine."

Amber hugged her daughter. "I am so proud to have a daughter like you."

They reached home to find Murad and his parents sitting in the front porch. Murad stood up smiling. He stretched out his arms and the two women walked into his enveloping embrace.

"I have some news for both of you."

"What news, Papa?" Nina asked.

"Neil called today to say he was offered a position as a trainee at the World Bank in Washington D.C. The bank gives out loans to developing countries. Its aim is to end world poverty. He will return home after his graduation, but he will need to move to Washington soon afterwards for this training program." Murad explained.

"Oh no! He has been gone for so long. I was looking forward to finally spending quality time with him."

"He'll be back home within six months. You can spend as much time as you want with him. This will be a good experience for him."

"I'm glad we'll all be together soon. With you and Neil not with us, for a while it seemed my family was partitioned!" Amber exclaimed.

Nina and Murad turned to hug Amber. "We will be a complete family, soon," Murad promised.

"What about you, Nina? You graduate this year. What do you want to do next? You loved to sing and play the harmonium. Have you been keeping up with your lessons?"

"I have, Papa. But what I'd really like to study are the new innovations in medicine. I want to be a doctor or a research scientist who studies diseases."

"That's great, then. Have you applied to the various colleges as yet?"

"We told her to apply to Lady Harding Medical College in New Delhi," said Murad's father. "It is an excellent school."

"I have applied there, Papa, but I haven't received a reply from the school."

"Send a follow up letter," Murad advised.

"You have more news to share, Murad. Tell Amber and Nina about it," Murad's mother urged.

"Yes, I talked to some of my friends today and I believe I have two jobs available for me. My friend, Hari, in Delhi, told me the government is looking to send a person to Hyderabad Sind, Pakistan, as the Indian High Commissioner and I fit the qualifications because I know many of the influential officials in Pakistan already and I have a background in finance and law.

The other offer was from my friend, Satish, who asked if I would like to join his international consultant company. This will mean moving to Delhi and will involve travel out of the country. You need to help me decide which offer I should accept or **if** I should accept them."

"You have just come back, Papa! You can't leave again. This is my last year at school. I'll be graduating soon. I can't move. And *Ammi* will need to complete her assignment at the school as well. Mother Superior won't be able to find a replacement for her so quickly. Just spend time with us for a while."

Murad glanced at Amber questioningly.

"Nina is right. We won't be able to leave Shimla till the end of this year. Why don't you delay your decision for a few days? Think about which of these offers suits you, and then make up your mind."

Epilogue
New Delhi, Hari and Sheila's Residence at the Palace of Jind October 1954
Murad and Amber's 25th Wedding Anniversary Party

The palace of Jind, the home of Hari and Sheila, was teeming with activity. Colorful *shamiyanas* or ceremonial tents were being erected on the main lawns. The side lawn had tables and chairs and a buffet table for the dinner after the ceremony. Hari and Sheila had graciously decided to offer their home for this event. The *halwai,* or cook, was setting up his table and pots to start the cooking process for tonight's dinner to celebrate Amber and Murad's twenty-fifth wedding ceremony. Lights decorated the trees and the palace. Marigold garlands decorated the hedges along the long driveway to the palace. Scented flowers perfumed the air. Water splashed from the fountain. The call of the birds provided a musical accompaniment. All around there was an air of anticipation and excitement. The palace had come to life.

"I have never seen anything so colorful," exclaimed George, Howard Skinner's son. He and his family had flown in from London just for this event.

Neil laughed. "My parents are only renewing their marriage vows during this ceremony. An actual Punjabi wedding celebration lasts a week. Punjabis are known to pull out all the stops. We are known for our liveliness, our music and our *bhangra* dancing.

"Renewing their vows is very important to your parents, isn't it?" George questioned.

"George, you know what happened to my family during the partition. We left Pakistan a few days before August 15 to move to Shimla. When my father followed a few days later, he lost his memory in an accident, and never made it across the border. The partition didn't just separate countries, it separated our family. When my parents met again after two and a half years, they went through a lot of ups and downs.

"By renewing their vows, they want to tell each other that they are ready to move forward with love and respect for each other," Neil replied. "They were going to do this privately, with just the family, but when they shared their thoughts with some of their friends, they insisted on a party!

"Uncle Hari called some of my parent's friends, and together, they are all hosting this affair!"

"I know," George nodded. "My dad couldn't wait to join in your parents happiness."

"Thank you for coming, George," Neil turned to hug his friend. "I am so grateful to your dad and your family for all your support. You are like my second family."

"How is it that your uncle Hari lives in a palatial mansion like this? Doesn't it belong to the Maharaja of Jind?"

"This palace does not belong to my Uncle Hari." Neil told George. "When the Princely States acceded to the Union of India in 1947, most of the Rajas and Maharajas gave away their forts, palaces, and land, to the government of India. Uncle Hari works for the government, and the ground floor of this palace has been leased to him. Many of the palaces have also been converted into government-run hotels."

"Thousands of people were killed during this partition. Hindus killed Muslims and Muslims killed Hindus. The partition seemed to foster so much hatred. Do you feel that the British are to blame for this, Neil?"

Neil thought about this question, surprised that it came from George, a British citizen. "The cost of the Partition is hard to imagine – almost a million died and ten million were left homeless. It was bad for the Muslims, Hindus, and Sikhs whose homeland was cut into two. But I don't think one can lay all the blame on the British. They had originally wanted a united India. They had seen the ability of Hindus and Muslims to live together for over a thousand years without conflict and bloodshed of this scale.

"As a matter of fact, India has always been accepting of different religions. Four major religions

Hinduism, Buddhism, Jainism, and Sikhism began here. India also welcomed people of all religions to settle here. We have Christians, Jews, Zoroastrians, and Baha'is, all living together. They follow their own belief systems. India has respected that."

"Do you think it was because the three leaders, Nehru, Gandhi, and Jinnah had an ideological and personality clash, and the British couldn't see them agree on a united or divided India?" asked George.

"That was definitely a big part of it," Neil replied.

"Well, I am glad that India is recovering from the chaos created by the partition."

They were interrupted by one of the relatives who wanted the boys to help him arrange some of the dinner tables. The boys helped happily stopping for a bit to get a snack from the *halwai*. Finally, as they saw the sun go down, they all decided to wash up and get dressed for the special event.

George smiled as he looked at the burnished sky. "I guess the sun does set on ..."

He didn't need to complete his sentence. They knew he was talking about the British Empire, which, at one time had been so vast, that at least one part of its territory was still in daylight.

***

Amber sat in the central courtyard, which was enclosed by the palace. Many of her friends sat around her while a beautician tended to Amber's makeup. She wore a beautiful blue chiffon sari, embellished with gold embroidery. The palms of her hands were adorned with beautiful henna designs.

"What are you thinking?" Ambika came from

behind, hugging her.

"I'm thinking how lucky I am to have good friends like you and Eric, and Sheila and Hari. I am so glad you could come."

"I wouldn't miss this event for anything. Eric and I have even planned a skit for after the ceremony," Ambika said.

"I know. Your children told me. It sounds hilarious. I can't wait," Amber replied with a smile.

"You must be so happy that your family is together again."

"Yes, Neil recently moved back home. He is working with the World Bank. Nina is attending a local medical college. Murad and I are together again," Amber smiled in reply.

"Murad and you have come a long way. Twenty-five years! You have seen so many changes in each other, and both of you have embraced those changes. It's great to see."

Amber's Reflections

Amber didn't tell her friend that they hadn't embraced the changes right away. After Murad's return from Pakistan, he had wanted everything to be the same as he had left it. But Amber had changed. She had become used to making decisions for her family. She had developed a confidence in her abilities and a 'take charge' attitude.

After their move to Delhi when Murad became a partner in his friend's international consulting company, he was not happy to hear that Amber had accepted a job with the Ministry of Education. The work of overseeing the building of new schools had seemed interesting to

Amber.

"You don't have to work anymore, Amber. I'm back. I work, and I can take care of all of us," Murad had protested.

"But I want to work. I don't have anything else to do. What do you want me to do all day, swat flies?"

"You have so many interests. You can explore your creative talents. We've just bought a new house. Make it a home with your feminine touch. I'm not saying you shouldn't do anything."

"Oh, so now I should go back to being a good housewife? We have a cook and housekeeper. Nina is in college. Neil works. Murad, you don't understand. I can make a difference in this job."

"Is that what you want?" Murad had jeered. "Be a career woman, focus on your job and forget that you have a husband who needs you? What do you suggest we do? Both of us work? Come home tired at the end of the day and have no time for each other? You wish I had never returned, don't you? Should I return to Pakistan and not come back?"

"You are twisting my words!" Tears had flooded her eyes, all the emotional turmoil inside her became too much to control.

"Oh, so is *this* how you'll handle all disagreements? Will you indulge in a display of tears when you are not getting your own way?"

"I *mourned* for you," Amber sobbed. "You don't have to attack me on a personal level. I am very happy we are together again, but you don't understand that I have changed. I need to do more with my life than housekeeping."

Murad had sighed impatiently. "I'm sorry. I was

thinking of you. I was thinking of us. I need you. I don't want to fight with you." His embrace was strong and warm. "I want you to be happy."

"And I want you to be happy as well," Amber replied. "It's just...sometimes I find your bossiness abrasive. But I love you, Murad. I really do," said Amber as she felt the pressure of his chin resting on her head. "And in the future, I promise to discuss all major decisions with you."

Murad smiled. "I call that communication, Amber."

They had many differences of opinion in the following years. But they had resolved them with love and laughter.

Amber remembered the Murad she had fallen in love with when she was nineteen years old. The idealistic, sweet, tender, and sophisticated Murad who taught her to dance, made her laugh, teased her, and loved her. The new Murad was more pragmatic, frank, and even be a little caustic. She had learned to accept and love those changes. Now, the more she tried to think of Murad as he was before, and how he had changed afterward, the more indivisible the two became.

With this discovery came the knowledge that her love for Murad was deep and enduring. He was the one man who saw her as a whole person. He saw her talents, doubts, and uncertainties.

***

"Congratulations," a warm, male voice interrupted her reverie. She looked up towards the voice.

"Nayan! How nice to see you!" A smile lit up Amber's face.

Nayan sucked in his breath. He stared at her,

cleared his throat and smiled. "I wish you and Murad every happiness," he told her huskily.

Nayan had connected again with Murad and Amber through his friend, Satish who was also Murad's business partner. Murad and Satish used Nayan's hotels to host their clients and Nayan always ensured that their guests got the best rooms and services he could provide. Nayan had been a successful hotelier when Amber had first met him, but now his hotels had achieved international acclaim.

"Thank you," Amber replied, looking at Nayan, her lustrous eyes glowing.

Thank you for bringing hope, joy, and laughter in my life. I didn't even realize I was dying a slow death after I heard the news of Murad's demise. Thank you for giving me a reason to live. Should she share her thoughts with Nayan? No, that would be inappropriate. Both Nayan and Rowena had taken her rejection of marriage to Nayan very well. Should she at least express her gratitude?

"Naya.."

But Nayan was already turning away from Amber. "I'll go congratulate Murad before the festivities begin. I believe he is in the next room." Nayan turned to walk away.

***

Murad donned his beautiful blue, brocade *shervani*, a long coat, and trousers that Amber had chosen for this occasion.

Neil walked in wearing his new outfit. "Papa, my skin itches under this *shervani*!"

"Are you wearing a shirt under it?" Murad asked turning to look at Neil.

205

"No, I didn't see any shirt with this *shervani*. I guess I can wear an older *kurta* under this prickly, brocade, coat. That will prevent my skin from chafing."

Eric, and Hari walked in just then. "Wow! Father and son look so handsome. Are you ready?" Hari exclaimed, "Your white horse awaits outside. The musicians are here as well."

Murad rolled his eyes. "You guys really decided to go all out. Amber and I were just planning on renewing our vows not re-enact the whole ceremony!"

They laughed.

"When a couple decides to make the same mistake twice, their friends want to be there to witness the occasion," joked Eric. "Seriously, though. This was a great idea. You are a lucky man. Amber is a beautiful woman."

Murad grinned. "I know I am. We have our differences but we understand each other."

Murad's Reverie

Murad had learned a lot from his relationship with Amber. He'd thought that a man's role was to protect his wife and family. He needed to be strong for them. He did not share his own thoughts and fears easily. Amber took this cue from him and treated him like her knight. He performed his role admirably.

He knew that as long as he took care of her, Amber would always be there for him. When they were together, Amber had never worked outside the home. Her job at the school in Shimla lasted only a few months after his return from Pakistan. In New Delhi, when Amber decided to work outside the home, he worried about losing her. He had displayed his fears

206

with anger. Amber had taught him that every person needed the freedom to choose and a sense of worthiness. She had taught him how important it was to share feelings and opinions. Now he could talk to her about anything, from some problem at work, to books, to politics. She had taught him how to love and respect a partner. He liked the way their relationship had evolved. Their differences had faded when they had stopped looking at each other for changes or flaws and had started looking forward together.

From the moment he'd met Amber, twenty-five years ago, he'd earmarked her as his, just as he had marked himself unavailable to any other but her. Yes, he was very ready to renew his marriage vows to the love of his life.

***

Murad climbed the white horse. Neil, his *sarwala* or groomsman, sat in front of him. Amber's uncle waited at the end of the long driveway of the Palace of Jind to help them dismount and guide them toward Amber.

Nina and Amber's friends led her to the garden where she awaited Murad, with a garland, to perform the *jai mala* ceremony. Grateful tears glistened in her eyes, and she smiled as she watched Murad, Neil, and the revelers approach. Fate had given her a second chance. Her life had everything she had ever wanted.

The band played their trumpets and drums loudly, while the groom's party danced the *bhangra* all the way. Murad smiled when he saw Amber. She looked more beautiful than ever.

A marriage relationship was like the bhangra, he mused, *once learned, the rhythm was never forgotten.*

Made in the USA
San Bernardino, CA
15 May 2016